The Christian Ministry Series

When I was a publisher I had the privilege of publishing the
I Believe Series and the Jesus Library, working with Michael Green
who was the series editor. It is now a still greater privilege to be
writing this foreword as the series editor for the new Christian
Ministry Series, designed to equip individual Christians and the
local church for effective ministry into the new millennium. The
Christian Ministry Series will explore a wide range of issues vital
for individual Christians and for the Church. The series is committed to excellence, with each book produced by a prominent leader
in their field. Every author will be asked to provide a bedrock of
stimulating biblical reflection, combined with a practical approach
designed to ensure that the particular dimension of Christian
ministry they are exploring has every opportunity to take off both
for individuals and within the local church.

While some will come to the series as a result of a book that
deals with their specialist ministries, we believe that many will
decide that the growing series is a resource that they cannot afford
to be without. The Christian Ministry Series will help readers to
develop and improve their present ministry but will also enable
many to branch out into areas they have never explored before.
We believe that many individual leaders and many local churches
will recognise the value of collecting the entire series, whether to
add to an existing range of resources or to begin an investment in
resources for effective ministry. In a world of constant and rapid
change, both in society and in the Church, the Christian Ministry
Series will take us back to the unchanging foundations of Scripture

and enable us to move forward with confidence and effectiveness. My prayer is that these books will release *maximum ministry* in many churches, not only in Britain but around the world.

Together We Stand was conceived over a meal beside the Sea of Galilee, eaten at sunset near to where Jesus may have eaten with his first disciples. After several days of prayer in the Galilean hills, Clive Calver and I had become aware of the need for a resounding restatement of evangelical convictions and identity. In order to resist the dangers of fragmentation into marginalised factions, and in order to seize the opportunities which will arise as the Western world faces up to the bankruptcy of secular materialism, we need to recognise anew the historic evangelical convictions that remain crucial and invigorating today. Only with a clear grasp of our identity and priorities do we have the potential and opportunity to make a real difference for Christ, both through the local church and in the nations. This book is therefore a clarion call to evangelicals not to lose sight of our foundational unity and to rally together in the cause of Christ. Biblical unity is the only adequate foundation for the effectiveness of all our ministries. Only together can we make a real impact upon our communities, our nations and the world. Our appeal is therefore the same as the Apostle Paul's:

If you have any encouragement from being united with Christ, if any comfort from his love, if any fellowship with the Spirit, if any tenderness and compassion, then make my joy complete by being like minded, having the same love, being one in spirit and purpose (Philippians 2:1–2).

Rob Warner
Queens' Road Church
Wimbledon
December 1995

Together We Stand

Clive Calver and Rob Warner

Hodder & Stoughton
LONDON SYDNEY AUCKLAND

British Library Cataloguing in Publication Data
A record for this book is available from the British Library

ISBN 0340 64237 8

Printed and bound in Great Britain by
Cox & Wyman Ltd, Reading, Berks

Hodder and Stoughton Ltd
A Division of Hodder Headline PLC
338 Euston Road
London NW1 3BH

This book is dedicated to
our dear wives,
Ruth and Claire,
who demonstrate the
grace, patience and wisdom
that is essential for us
to be able to say that
together we stand

Contents

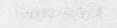

Foreword

'I can't see who's leading, but it's either Oxford or Cambridge.' So spoke veteran commentator John Snagge to the British public many years ago as he peered through the water-streaked windscreen of the BBC launch that was following the rowers in the Oxford and Cambridge Boat Race. It was one of radio's classic bloopers. I was reminded of it as I read through *Together We Stand*.

Not that you see here slips of the pen matching John Snagge's slip of the tongue – Clive Calver and Rob Warner are careful writers. But, like John Snagge, they are following something that is not easy to see, just because it moves fast and throws spray as it goes along. Their book comes out of the currently seething pot of English evangelicalism, which they are trying to monitor and also direct in a way that expresses their identification with it as well as their anxieties about it. Their excitement at evangelical expansion is tempered with anxiety as they spot cracks in the wall of the large complex that is currently going up. Although since 1979 my shoes have been 6,000 miles away from theirs, I hope it makes sense for me to say that in their shoes I should feel the same.

Half a century ago, when spiritually I began to sit up and take notice, evangelicals in England had the status of an eccentric Protestant minority. There were not many of them, and they kept themselves to themselves in a loose defensive association fed by interdenominational magazines, mission interests at home and abroad, and convention meetings. On Sundays they worshipped either as low-church prayer-book Anglicans or in the hymn-sandwich Free Church frame or in the lead-passing style of the

Brethren; there was no fourth option. The routines did not change, and the spirit of Laodicea was unquestionably abroad. But today England is estimated to have at least three times as many evangelicals as before (a million and a quarter at the last count), charismatic renewal has left its mark everywhere, new churches and new music have appeared, denominational uniformities have broken up, skeleton jazz combos lead folk-type worship sing-songs, tens of thousands march for Jesus, and Spring Harvest serves up to ninety thousand people annually. With all this new vitality – which is wonderful – the centrifugal Corinthian temper, zealous, quarrelsome, triumphalist, super-spiritual, judgmental, complacent, unstable, seems to be raising its head. The tidiness of sedate death is giving way to the untidiness of immature life. It is a good problem to have to deal with but, as Paul found long ago, it is indeed a problem.

The Calver–Warner combine sees the internal unity of evangelicalism as increasingly at risk, just because God's truth is today on fire in so many ardent but imperfectly sanctified hearts. The writers see the role of the Evangelical Alliance as promoter of unity, comity, sanity and charity in this scene as something of importance, and surely they are right, just as they are right to affirm that, though the national spiritual temperature has risen, revival has not come yet. Their tract for the times – for that is what this book is – merits serious attention and some humble rethinking as a response, and I hope this is what it will receive.

J. I. PACKER
Regent College
Vancouver, BC
Canada

See how these Christians love one another

The queue stretched right down the aisle of the church building. Older and younger Christians waiting silently in a line to take pieces of bread from the table at the front. Then, one by one, they handed a piece of bread to someone else. Their murmured words of apology and quiet prayers magnified the sense of subdued awe at what was happening in that place. The challenge had been simple: 'If you have something against someone here take them a piece of bread. If you have failed to encourage an individual here ... if you need forgiveness from somebody ... if you want to commit yourself to pray for another person ... then take them a piece of bread and begin there.'

The preacher's theme had been straightforward. We need to love each other, to demonstrate our commitment to one another, because Jesus commanded it – and because the world requires proof of who we claim to be. The sharing of bread was to be no more than a symbol to accompany words and prayers of forgiveness, repentance and mutual acceptance.

The response had been swift. First one person rose, then another, then another – and one could hear the sharp communal intake of breath as certain individuals joined the queue. It was unnatural, only the Holy Spirit could engineer such a reply. For this was no impersonal, anonymous city-wide congregation. It was a village community, drawn from three separate churches, that had no contact with each other. The majority of the members of these three congregations had refused to pass more than common

civilities for thirty years! It is hard to imagine the extent of the
damage that had been inflicted upon Christian witness in that little
community. For hostility, or even indifference, between churchgoers does not pass unnoticed by others within a secular society.

Sadly this is not an isolated illustration. Indeed, it has even been
suggested that one verse of the old hymn, 'Onward Christian
Soldiers', could have been rewritten in the 1960s to reflect the
situation then, in a more accurate fashion. It would then read

> We are all divided,
> Not one body we,
> One lacks faith, another hope,
> And all lack charity.[1]

Too often the allegation is levelled by non-Christian observers that
we are little more than hypocrites. We claim to have received the
love of Jesus Christ in our lives, but often do little to illustrate this
fact in our relationships with one another. This alone may help to
explain why so many people in modern society claim a high regard
for Jesus Christ alongside a general dislike for the organised church
which bears his name.

Jesus himself ordained that the way in which the world would
know who he is does not lie in the propagation of doctrine –
however correct it might be! Nor does it lie in the efficacy of our
traditions, or the performance of significant rituals. Instead Christian truth is to be demonstrated by the way in which we love and
care for each other. It is our unity, that sense of shared 'togetherness' which vindicates the truth of the message we proclaim. Jesus
boldly announced that, 'By this all men will know that you are my
disciples, if you love one another' (John 13:35). This was no
unachievable pipe-dream. Just 150 years after the death of Jesus
the church historian Tertullian was able to record an amazing
statement from pagan observers. While accusing the Christians of
atheism, and misunderstanding the communion and love-feasts as
bouts of cannibalism and drunken orgies, they kept saying in
amazement, 'See how these Christians love one another'.

If Christianity were simply a religion to which mental assent
alone were required, then there would be room within it for those
with cold, unfeeling hearts. It is not. Christian truth comes from a

solid, firm doctrinal basis rooted in the clear teaching of inspired Scripture. But real Christianity can never be reduced to a mere academic acceptance of its propositions. The central question can never be 'What do we know about Jesus in our heads?', but 'What does he mean to us in our hearts?' For to know Jesus is never to merely affirm what we know about him, but to register the changes brought to us by his transforming love in our lives. Because Christianity is a relationship with God rather than merely a religion about him, it *must* transcend the level of words alone. Therefore our love for one another must similarly surpass a mere lip-service to the principles of unity, our commitment together must become an experienced and observable part of our church life today.

What is this Church?

Few people within Western society would regard the Church as likely to hold any surprises for them. Yet the moment the impartial observer begins to explore the true nature and character of the Church that Jesus founded the results prove very surprising.

The most obvious impression created by that single word 'Church' is of a particular kind of building. Usually the image conveyed is of a Gothic construction, with steeple and bells, or of a Victorian chapel with its rigid pews and stuffy atmosphere. Even that architectural stereotype may be somewhat out of date. For most growing churches have adapted at least the interior of their buildings to provide a more relaxed and welcoming context for worship.

But the New Testament never equated 'Church' with a building. The most obvious reason for this was the fact that ecclesiastical buildings did not exist. For the first three centuries of its existence Christianity was an illegal religion within the Roman Empire. To construct a building for Christian worship would never have been permitted – and yet that era saw the greatest period of numerical witness that the Church has witnessed until the present day. The word 'Church' did not refer to an institution or rigid structure either. The most commonly used Greek word for 'Church' is *ekklesia* and it always referred to 'people', never to a structure.

This word was not invented by the early Christians. It was a term they borrowed from secular Greek society where it was used to refer to a public meeting. The *ekklesia* was a forum where civic leaders would explain their plans to the people in order to enlist their support and listen to the grievances and objections of the citizens. When such a meeting was called people were called out to gather for it by a blast on a trumpet. The literal meaning was therefore 'called out', so when Christians adopted the word they were referring to themselves as a 'called out' people.

When the Hebrew Old Testament had been translated into Greek for the Septuagint version in around 200 BC, two Hebrew words *edah* and *qahal* were translated as *ekklesia*. These were used to describe any meeting of the entire Israelite nation, whether for worship, reading the law, politics, or even to discuss the idea of revolution! (Numbers 13:26–14:10). It was particularly employed when Israel was summoned together to meet with God (see Numbers 10:7; Deuteronomy 4:10; Judges 20:2; Psalms 107:32). So the word acquired a religious connotation.

The church is therefore a called out people. For *ekklesia* breaks down into two parts, *ek* out of, and *klesis* calling. We are called 'out of darkness into his wonderful light' (1Peter 2:9). So the church is about people, not bricks; it is an organism rather than an organisation.

When the scholar William Tyndale became the first person to translate the Bible from Hebrew and Greek into English, he consistently translated *ekklesia* as 'congregation'.

This emphasis on 'people' rather than 'buildings' was over-turned eighty years later in 1611, by the translators of the Authorised Version. They used 'church' instead of 'congregation' as their rendering of *ekklesia*. They did this despite the fact that the English word 'church' and the Scottish term 'kirk' stem from another Greek word *kyriakon*, which means 'the Lord's house'. It is perhaps from this unfortunate translation that our building-centred fixation has come. In order to understand properly our essential unity as a Church we need to recover the fact that the Church is people, not a construction in which we meet. Our unity is not a coming-together of buildings or structures, but of people who have committed their lives to love and serve the Lord Jesus Christ.

There is one sense in which the church is a building

(1Corinthians 3:9–7; Ephesians 2:19–22; 1Peter 2:4–8), but we are the bricks. God has not chosen to live in temples built by people, but among his people (Matthew 18:20; John 14:23; Acts 7:48, 17:24). Those visiting the church should not see a human construction but witness the fact that God has chosen to live within ordinary people (1Corinthians 3:16).

The people of God began as wandering nomads exploring the wilderness. During this period God was prepared to inhabit a tent – this became the place of God's presence. Then the death and resurrection of Jesus ushered in a whole new era, our God no longer dwells under canvas – he now lives in us as his people and his Church (1Peter 2:5).[2]

It is no coincidence that some of the most outstanding examples of church growth, as in China, have taken place in the absence of recognised 'places of worship'. The same was true for the early church. Because there were no church buildings, apart from the Jewish synagogues, Christians usually met together in their homes (Romans 16:5; 1Corinthians 16:19; Colossians 4:15; Philemon v.2).

When persecution against the Christians grew, many local congregations were forced to seek unlikely alternative accommodation. The church in Rome even used parts of the subterranean cemetery known as 'the catacombs'. Similarly, in Britain today, as a number of churches have enjoyed considerable numerical expansion, or as 'new churches' have been established which have rejected the economic implication of acquiring property, churches will meet in school halls, community centres or even the 'upper rooms' of public houses. The argument behind such practice is simple: buildings may be helpful, or provide a visible landmark, but their only significance is as a meeting place for the church.

One church I visited had felt the need to purchase suitable premises for their local congregation. Instead of erecting an 'ecclesiastical' building they built a sports hall. The badminton court could be easily adapted into a sanctuary for Sunday worship. During the rest of the week their facilities did not need to remain idle and unused. They provided excellent resources for both church and community – and also broke down any reluctance on the part of non-Christians to set foot in a church building. They saw nothing inconsistent in this. By rejecting the idea that architecture should be 'sacred', this utilitarian structure significantly removed barriers from the local community – and the church grew!

For too long society has retained a caricature of the church as a Gothic mausoleum within which God is worshipped through outdated rituals and practices. The transformation that has taken place in many of our buildings, and much of our worship, must be matched by a change in our demonstration of what it means to be 'church' within our locality. Many individuals are not seeking somewhere to visit, but for something relevant to which to belong. The challenge that we face is to recapture that sense of community which lay at the heart of the early church. We must confront the issue: with whom does our unity lie – the people with whom we share a building, or all those in whose lives God has also made his home?

What is this unity?

Evangelical Christians have always maintained a particular obsession with individuality. Some of this owes its origin to the understanding of personal conversion. Yet while this is individual at the beginning it is the entry into a community. While the word 'saint' is used only once in Scripture, 'saints' occurs no less than 61 times.

As individuals God gives us his Spirit, but collectively he gives us each other. It is vital that we recognise that, apart from the Holy Spirit, the greatest gift we receive from God is one another. For we were never meant to have to struggle along solo, instead we were designed to be indispensable to each other. This point is strongly maintained by the Apostle Paul when he insists that we are the people of God, and individually members of Christ's body (1Corinthians 12:12, 27). The analogy he draws is a vivid one, because no single person is the body of Christ, that identity is a collective provilege. The picture is not of an arm, some toes, an ear and legs desperately seeking to unite together. Instead under Christ as our head, we naturally fit together to form a unit suitable for him to operate in and through as his body.

Just as eyes need ears and vice versa, so we remain incomplete when apart from each other (1Corinthians 12:15–20). This offers us a clear illustration of unity in diversity. We are not designed to be the same as each other, nor to perform identical functions, but we are inextricably linked to each other. The only possible division would be created by amputation, if we were forcibly cut off from the rest of the body.

We are therefore 'one' body just as God is 'one' (1Timothy 2:5). The Old Testament insists that there is one God (Deuteronomy 6:4). This one God is the creator and sustainer of life. Paul argues that because of the unity of God we should enjoy unity. He urged that, 'There is one body and one Spirit; just as you were called to one hope when you were called – one Lord, one faith, one baptism, one God and Father of us all, who is over all and through all and in all' (Ephesians 4:4–6).

Similarly there is one God in the one Lord Jesus Christ. We must recognise that, 'In a Christian sense no one can speak of God unless he is speaking concretely of Jesus'.[3] He is one with God the Father (John 10:30; 17:11, 21). This Jesus is the one Lord, introducing one faith and one baptism (Ephesians 4:5). The foundation and continuity of the Church's unity are grounded in Jesus as the one shepherd of one flock (John 10:14).

There is also one God in the one Spirit of Christ. Jews and Gentiles are united together by Jesus, 'for through Him we both have access to the Father by one Spirit' (Ephesians 2:18). It is this same Holy Spirit who provides gifts for the Church and their variety is harmonised only as we operate in the unity that the Spirit gives (1Corinthians 12:9–11). However, the gifts that we have been given will differ from each other. God has not designed a monochrome picture, but incorporates a glorious variety of talents and abilities among his people. In recognising the different ministries which he gives we are instructed to use these in the service of one another. We each make our individual contribution and God can bless the totality for he puts the pieces of the jigsaw together into a complete picture.

The gifts that we have may not always be the ones that we would have wished for. From the moment of my father's conversion in his late teens he longed to be a preacher. At times he occupied a pulpit, people seemed to appreciate what he shared, but little of dynamic significance seemed to emerge. Often he would join others preaching in the open air, but few stopped to listen. Even as a child I came to the sober realisation that my dad was not going to be a renowned speaker. This was not something that dad found easy to accept, for he longed that God would use him in this way.

Some years later I was planning, with my friend Peter Meadows (now of Premier Radio), a meeting which we were going to hold in the Royal Albert Hall. We desperately required someone who could run the box-office for us, and sell tickets through the months preceding the event. Knowing that as a station manager for British Rail my father had to understand the ramifications of railway timetables I thought the seating-plan from the Albert Hall was not beyond him! I well remember seeing Peter shaking his head with amazement after the event had proved to be very successful. His sense of wonder was not induced by the excellent preaching and music of that evening, nor by the number who had come to faith in Christ that night. It was just a source of genuine surprise that my dad had engineered everyone into the right seat for the event, and for the overspill performance that had to be arranged for the afternoon!

Subsequently my father's support was enlisted for a tour of thirteen venues that we were planning for the next year. He was reluctant but agreed on condition that he could take time off work and travel with us in order to supervise the box-office in each location.

One night he spoke to me with tears in his eyes and said, 'Tonight I heard Luis Palau preach as I could never preach, I watched Dave Pope lead worship and listened to Graham Kendrick sing in a fashion that I could never emulate. I watched people giving their lives to Christ in a way I have never seen. But I sensed the Lord telling me that while I could never do these things, the people whose lives were being changed would never even be here without the gift he had given to me.' Three months later he died. But I knew that my dad had discovered that God does not just give gifts to preachers, he loves administrators too!

Our gifts will be different, but when they are harmoniously combined with one another the body of Christ is seen in operation. This is why Paul insists that there must be unity in the church. It is simply because 'there is one body and one spirit' (Ephesians 4:4). The word – *henotes* – unity, only occurs in his epistle to the Ephesians. This majestic word expresses that mature unity of faith, given by the Holy Spirit, which is always needed to demonstrate the true life and character of the church (Ephesians 4:3,13).

Unity in the New Testament is always viewed from the perspective of Jesus Christ. He alone is the Lord, the revelation of God to humankind (Acts 4:12; 1Corinthians 8:4; 1Timothy 2:5). The believer's union with Christ is not a physical one, it is a spiritual unity (1Corinthians 6:17). We are brothers and sisters, united in the body of Christ through the Holy Spirit (1Corinthians 12:12; Galatians 3:28; Ephesians 4:4; Colossians 3:15; Hebrews 2:11).

In the picture of the Church as the body of Christ we see the basic idea of unity, but this does not consist of us all being submerged into one vast amorphous mass.

Within the one being of God there are three equal persons, Father, Son and Holy Spirit. These three relate to each other in a relationship marked out by self-giving love (John 16:14; 17:4,24; 1Corinthians 2:10). At the heart of the Christian faith lies an attitude of simple faith and trust in a God who is not only personal, but who exists as a loving community of equal persons. God himself is a family of Father, Son and Holy Spirit. The love that exists in this family is eternal, it is a basic part of the divine character (1John 4:8). At the centre of the universe we find not a solitary, lonely deity, but a God who rejoices in relationships.

What is this family?

It has often been pointed out that while we can choose our friends we are not at liberty to select our relatives. Nowhere is this more true than in the Church. For it is a simple fact that from the moment we surrender the control of our lives to Jesus Christ He not only comes to live within us by his Holy Spirit, but also incorporates us into his family – the Church. We therefore do not merely share a common faith with Christian colleagues, but become brothers and sisters together. It is possible to disagree over mutually exclusive forms of baptism, methods of church government or styles of worship, but we still retain a shared identity as family together. We might not have chosen each other, or always approve of one another, but we certainly are not allowed to reject other family members.

Scripture points to only *one* people of God, '*the* Church'. This consists of all true believers, those who have come through repentance and faith, to trust in Jesus Christ for their salvation. This is the great equalising truth – whatever our race, class, education, gender or background, we are all sinners for whom Jesus Christ has died (Romans 3:23; 8:32). Each one of us becomes a believer, not though any good deeds of our own but simply because of the grace and kindness of crucified love. We are therefore 'all one in Christ Jesus' (Galatians 3:28). We are one in our relationship with the Father, now part of the family, and so brothers and sisters in Jesus Christ.

When he instructed Mary Magdalene after his resurrection, to return to his disciples Jesus called them brothers for the first time. He did not say that he was then going to 'our father', but to 'my father and your father' (John 20:17). The meaning is straight-forward, Jesus was the only begotten Son and therefore co-equal with his Father (John 3:16) – we are adopted children, brought by Jesus into the family to be together with him.

It is therefore strange to note that when we speak of 'church' today we are more likely to be speaking of an individual member of the family, rather than the family itself. Today there are over 22,000 denominations in the world, with five new ones added each week![4] When we talk about the Baptist Church or the Church of England we are just not talking in biblical terms.

For Paul and the other New Testament writers there were not many churches, but one Church. It is true that local churches did exist in various towns and cities. Yet these did not regard themselves as operating in isolation from each other. Their co-operation was expressed by sharing in each other's need and receiving ministry from one another (Acts 2:42–5; 4:34, 6:1–6; Romans 15:25–6). They recognised that the message of the Holy Spirit to the church in one locality was relevant to others as well (1Corinthians 4:17; 1Thessalonians 2:14). They knew that they possessed a genuine spiritual unity in Christ, he was the head of the Church, and in each place their accountability was to him (Acts 4:46, 4:11,32). The final reality of the church as they perceived it was that it was not local or regional but the universal body of people who have been redeemed by Jesus Christ. There-fore although there were many local churches, they all saw themselves as small parts of the whole Church throughout the world (Ephesians 2:19–22; 5:23–32; 1Timothy 3:15; Hebrews 12:22–4).

The Church is therefore not merely the body of believers in one place, but the family of all true Christian believers, past, present and future.

Christian leaders through the centuries have, however, drawn a distinction between the visible and the invisible church. Today some 1.78 billion people are visibly attached to the Church worldwide. Some of these will only be nominal Christians, the invisible Church is the real Church, the care of true believers, and it is more difficult to place real numbers on them. It was Augustine of Hippo who made this point when he emphasised that 'there are many sheep without, many wolves within', but he was merely echoing what Jesus himself had taught in the parable of the wheat and the tares (Matthew 13:24–30, 36–43).

In the mind of God there is no such thing as a Lutheran, Methodist, Anglican, Pentecostal or even a Free Church, and in heaven all extraneous labels will disappear. It will probably also be populated by many people who we personally feel should never have been allowed through the gates! There will be differences of opinion among evangelicals over the need for denominations. Some will echo the words of John Noble, 'Father, forgive us our denominations as we forgive those who denomination against us'. Others will see denominations as representative only of style and emphasis maintaining that they only represent the existence of variety in the body of Christ. Some will concur with the judgement of the late J. P. Baker that, 'Denominational groupings, existing over and against one another in the same place, are rank denial of the Church's nature and character as *the* Church of Christ'.[5] Either way it is tragic to recognise how easily the Church has become divided when secondary issues or political considerations have become more important than our basic and vital unity centred on Christ and the salvation he brings. The only natural ground for dividing the Church into separate congregations in the New Testament is that of geography.

It is therefore of critical importance that we do not allow our particular emphases which are not involved with the integrity of the Gospel to compromise our unity. It has been encouraging to note a growing trend towards evangelical unity which has taken place in recent decades, for our oneness and mutual support and love for each other must constitute a basic witness to the truth of the Gospel message we proclaim.

The mutual commitment in a family unit can normally be tested by the way in which its members treat each other. This will be of especial significance in the Church for we are not only family members, our destiny is to reign for eternity as the bride of Christ (Revelation 19:6–9; 21:2,9; 22:17).

The Bible points to our spiritual intimacy with Christ. With great daring Jesus employed the word 'know', which is often used in Scripture for the sexual relationship of a married couple, to describe our relationship with God (John 17:3). In return we are assured that God delights in us, as a bridegroom rejoices in his bride (Isaiah 62:5). If we are to reign as the bride of Christ then we need to be ready for that moment.

I have to confess to taking great personal pleasure from conducting weddings, and one stands out in my memory as a never-to-be-forgotten occasion. I had just instructed the bridegroom and best man to be ready for the bride's arrival. She was due at any moment so I suggested that it would be good for them to stand together in the aisle. When the bride had walked to within a few feet of the bridegroom the best man should nudge the bridegroom so that he could turn and smile in encouragement at his bride. I figured that as they would be sitting opposite each other at the breakfast table for the next few decades she would need all the encouragement available! As she came up the aisle I stared in horror! For the woman the bridegroom was supposed to be marrying was a delightful Christian, but unlikely to win a beauty contest. The woman approaching me, in contrast, looked absolutely stunning!

I wondered at what would happen – we clearly had the wrong person, and at any moment the bridegroom would turn and be faced with an unexpected decision! Only as she drew nearer did I recognise the father, and then it dawned on me that this was the right woman – only on her wedding day she looked absolutely radiant! The bridegroom turned and smiled, and as he looked back at me I saw the word 'Cor!' on his lips.

The simple fact is that Jesus is coming back to marry us – his church, and take us to be his bride. He is not returning for a poor, haggard old woman, who feebly hobbles up the aisle in a filthy wedding garment. He is coming for a bride who is fit for a king! The challenge to the Church is to be ready for the bridegroom's return. To be so in love with Jesus, and with each other, that we will be an appropriate bride – ready for the occasion.

This means that our relationships must be right with each other. As one analyst suggests, 'The first focus of New Testament teaching on Church unity is the teaching that genuine unity among Christians is primarily a *relational* unity (love and harmony) rather than a focus on *organisational* unity (external connectedness) within the church'.[6] Jesus made the acceptance of God's word as truth an intrinsic requirement for such unity (John 17:6–8, 17). For too long it has been true that,

> To the outsider the word 'church' all too often conjures up an odd and unhelpful collection of ideas; a cold, formal, uninviting building; archaic and unintelligible services; boring, lengthy and irrelevant teaching; strangely dressed men remote from everyday life and often appealing for money; a bevy of bishops, dignitaries and councils; middle-class 'do-gooders' and escapist hypocrites; denominations staying apart and suspicious of each other.[7]

We may legitimately ask if this was the type of church that Christ came to build, or the kind of people with whom he intends to spend eternity? For the divine architect is not merely preparing for a building for today. The dust, dirt and confusion of much that makes up contemporary Church life may resemble a building-site, but God's intention is a finished product that will be a people fit and ready to be his dwelling place for eternity.

The challenge to us is simple and direct – get ready!

2

One in the Spirit

The vast ballroom was packed with people. Each had come with a different expectation, yet everyone knew that this was a time for celebration. To meet with God, to listen to his word, and sing his praises.

On the distant stage a strong Welsh voice asked basic questions, 'How many of you here are committed Christians?' 'Do you love Jesus and seek to live in relationship with him under the direction of the Bible?' Almost every hand was raised in response to affirm his, or her, Christian convictions. But then came another question. 'How many of you would admit to being an evangelical?' Consternation and confusion reigned. Many were unsure what the question meant, and were uncertain as to what their response should be. The word was not unfamiliar but its precise meaning was unclear. Some hands shot up in recognition of what they believed. Many wavered until about one in three had their hands in the air. Two out of three remained uncertain.

'An evangelical is a person who has committed his, or her, life to Jesus Christ, seeking to live under his Lordship and authority, believing and accepting the Bible for what it says.' A murmur spread through the hall. Relief replaced consternation, shame at their ignorance and surprise that the answer should be so simple and straightforward.

Evangelical Christians have largely been passing through a twentieth-century identity crisis. Many have been in danger of losing their roots, or at least of forgetting where they originated. To lose touch with our heritage is to threaten both our identity and the nature of our unity, but many contemporary evangelicals are unaware of how the evangelical tradition is rooted in history.

Retracing our footsteps

It is currently fashionable among religious pundits and media correspondents to regard evangelicalism as a modern movement. Its origins are traced to the emergence of fundamentalism in the early years of the twentieth century. This view may be popular but it is totally fictitious.

Evangelicals were alive and well in the nineteenth century, and earlier. Spontaneous outbursts of evangelistic fervour as in the missions of Phoebe Palmer and D. L. Moody existed alongside the passionate social involvement of George Muller, William Wilberforce, Lord Shaftesbury and Doctor Barnardo. The twin streams united in the flamboyant independence of the Salvation Army and the caring missionary outreach of men like William Carey, Hudson Taylor and Henry Martyn. All were convinced evangelicals. They, and thousands of others like them, were not ashamed to acknowledge the impetus given by the Great Evangelical Awakening of the eighteenth century.

On 24 May 1738, John Wesley, an Anglican clergyman who felt a failure in his abortive mission to the Americans, wrote these words:

I felt my heart strangely warmed, I felt I did trust in Christ, Christ alone for salvation; and an assurance was given me that He had taken away my sins, even mine, and saved me from the law of sin and death.[1]

This experience proved to be the turning point of his ministry. He travelled a quarter of a million miles on horseback, preached over forty thousand sermons and challenged ordinary men and women, gathered in the open air, to turn from their sinful lives and acknowledge Jesus Christ as their Saviour and Lord. Despite severe criticism, opposition and presecution, John Wesley, George Whitefield and many others, preached the Gospel to half the British population. To a society that had faced warfare, rationalist philosophy and severe extremes of poverty, their message offered hope for the future. Historians have suggested that Britain avoided the conflagration that engulfed their near neighbours in the French Revolution because the Evangelical Revival offered a life-changing revolution of a different kind for ordinary working people.

Many evangelicals have chosen to trace their beliefs to this Evangelical Awakening; but the roots of evangelicalism stretch even further beyond the eighteenth century.

European evangelicals look to the pietist movement of the seventeenth century. Their emphasis on personal faith contributed to the growth of the Moravian church whose leader, Jan Amos Comenius, wrote to other 'evangelical churches'. Moravian refugees found shelter on the estates of Count Zinzendorf. There they erected a building on a hill they renamed 'Herrnhut' (the Lord's Watch). They established a prayer meeting which continued, nonstop, for 100 years. Moravian missionaries spread throughout Europe, one of whom, Peter Bohler, convinced John Wesley and his brother, Charles, of their need to be justified by faith in Jesus Christ.

These European movements had their own roots in the sixteenth-century Reformation which divided the Church into Protestant and Catholic traditions. The Protestant movement and its Puritan successors, regarded themselves as evangelical believers. Recognising that membership of the Church was insufficient grounds for personal salvation, they spoke of an individual being justified (made right) with God through faith in his Son Jesus.

The author of the English *Book of Common Prayer*, Thomas Cranmer, wrote in 1537 of '*one sound, pure, evangelical doctrine, conformable to the discipline of the primitive church*'. In similar vein, Martin Luther affirmed that '*A truly evangelical man would not run here and there, he will stick to truth to the end*'. Often German-speaking people would use the words, 'reformer' or 'evangelical' interchangeably. Their favourite self-description was '*die Evangelischen*' meaning 'Evangelical men'. The Elector of Saxony used the word 'evangelical' to distinguish between those who were true believers and others who were no more than Christian humanists. Luther wrote in 1522 of 'this common evangelical cause'. He used the term evangelical because he was horrified that his followers were called by his name. Gradually 'reformer' and 'evangelical' came to be used interchangeably.

But were there evangelicals before the Reformation? The first date given by the Oxford English Dictionary for the use of the word 'evangelical' is 1532. Yet previously the dominant religious languages were Latin and Greek. The first use of the term in England dates back at least as far as John Wyclif in the fourteenth century. He was named '*Doctor Evangelicus*', and at the time of his death in 1384 left an unfinished work: *Opus Evangelicum*.

Evangelical Christians trace their spiritual lineage through the mystical and spiritual countercultures of the mediaeval and early Church. This is done through great thinkers such as Bernard, Anselm, Augustine, Athanasius and Irenaeus. Others look to minority religious movements who resisted corruption and the perversion of the primitive gospel within the ecclesiastical hierarchy of their times. They often incurred persecution from those within the institutional church authorities. So both within and beyond the established Roman Catholic and Eastern Orthodox churches, there were those who maintained and encouraged those distinctive attitudes which would today be broadly termed 'evangelical'.

The root word was first used in the early Church as the Latin adjective '*evangelicus*'. In the fourth century, Augustine used it to declare that '*the blood of the Christians is, as it were, the seed of the fruit of the Gospel*' (*semen fructum evangelicorum*).

Though the antiquity of the evangelical position may be a hindrance to some, for others its origins are reassuring. It is not a new innovation in theological thought. In fact, evangelicals would claim that their distinctiveness originates from the theology of the Apostle Paul and, ultimately in the teaching of Jesus himself. As John Stott has bluntly expressed it:

It is the contention of evangelicals that they are plain Bible Christians, and that in order to be a biblical Christian it is necessary to be an evangelical Christian. Put that way, it sounds arrogant and exclusive, but this is a sincerely held belief. Certainly it is the earnest desire of evangelicals to be neither more nor less than biblical Christians . . . If evangelical theology is biblical theology, it follows that it is not a new-fangled 'ism', a modern brand of Christianity, but an ancient form, indeed the original one. It is New Testament Christianity.[2]

Replying to the critics

One of the basic problems that evangelicals face today lies in the fact that words can become unpopular, and often can take on new forms of meaning. Certainly the word 'evangelical' has come in for more than its fair share of abuse, rejection and misinterpretation. There are many people who blatantly misuse the term – often through ignorance, although on occasions the motivation can stem from either malice or indifference.

There are many within society who would regard both Christianity and the Church as irrelevant to life in the modern world. Some will be hostile to Christianity, others merely display apathy towards it. For such people 'evangelical' was once a non-word, today it can often provoke a reaction! Evangelicals have come to be widely regarded as being excessive in their beliefs, fanatical in their attempts to persuade others, and extreme in their worship. They have adopted feelings and emotions with which to replace human reason.

Major objections fall into these areas:

(a) *Enthusiasm* – there is nothing new in this accusation. It was levelled against John Wesley and the early Methodists in the eighteenth century. Most British observers of religion concentrate on its established, institutional form, there is little regard for a faith which is orientated around spontaneous, demonstrative worship.

When Dr George Carey was appointed Archbishop of Canterbury the *Evening Standard* was disdainful in its dismissal of evangelicalism. It remarked that,

> The evangelical wing of the Church, to which he belongs, is notorious for packing them in with banjos, guitars, saxophones, synthesisers and dancing around the altar, but few of those who attend its ecclesiastical gigs are genuinely or lastingly converted to Christianity.[3]

Unfortunately this correspondent failed to record what research, statistical or otherwise, had been engaged in to substantiate this claim.

(b) *Fundamentalism* – evangelicals are often dismissively rejected as 'fundamentalists'. This notion has confused many, because it falls into the same category of error as the assumption that the Labour Party of the 1980s was exactly the same as the Militant Tendency (its more extreme left-wing faction). It was true that, until their expulsion, all members of the Militant Tendency were part of the Labour Party, but not all members of the Labour Party were allied to the Militant Tendency!

In the same way all fundamentalists are evangelical, but the majority of British evangelicals would not accept a 'fundamentalist' label. For fundamentalism concentrates upon its hostility towards modern theology, places its major emphasis on the total inerrancy of the Bible, is negative towards any form of Biblical criticism, and believes that those who do not share its views are not really Christians.[4]

Evangelicals will have some sympathy with these perspectives but will not take them as far as fundamentalists would wish. The contrast may be simply represented as in the table on p. 20.[5]

(c) *Moralism* – evangelicals are frequently regarded as being concerned with moral issues like sexuality, family and pornography, at the expense of others. The picture is one of an aggrieved 'auntie' remonstrating with the moral laxity perceived in today's society, yet impervious to the pain of the homeless or unemployed in Britain, and to the thousands dying of starvation worldwide.

It is true to observe that many evangelicals, at the turn of the twentieth century, were guilty of having mislaid their social conscience. Their nineteenth-century predecessors had been actively involved in the campaign against slavery, in philanthropic acts towards the poor, orphaned and destitute, and in seeking Parliamentary redress for social ills. Yet twentieth-century evangelicalism was content to focus on seeking to 'save souls'. This amnesia was partly a result of the rise of liberal theology and the subsequent emphasis on the so-called 'social gospel'. Evangelicals reacted and viewed with suspicion any activity that could not be regarded as direct evangelism.

FUNDAMENTALISTS	EVANGELICALS
* Are suspicious of scholarship and science. Tend to be anti-intellectual.	* Encourage academic study in order to develop a deeper understanding of faith.
* Have a 'mechanical' view of how the Bible was written.	* Believe it essential to understand the culture and circumstances in which the Bible was written.
* Believe the Authorised (King James) Version as the only inspired translation.	* Value the Authorised Version, but believe there are now more accurate translations.
* Have literalistic approach to interpreting the Bible.	* See the Bible as a rich collection of history, poetry, prophecy, metaphor and symbol – to be understood accordingly.
* Reject involvement with Christians who do not accept their views.	* Will not negotiate on the essentials of Christian faith. But believe secondary differences do not prevent co-operation with others.
* Often allow their culture to influence their beliefs. Thus, some support racial intolerance, 'prosperity teaching' and politically 'right-wing' views.	* Seek to allow the Bible to question and challenge culture – including their own.
* Have denied, until recently, that the Christian gospel has social implications.	* Believe that Christians have a duty to be 'salt and light' in society.
* Insist on certain views concerning the Second Coming of Christ.	* Believe there are legitimate differences of interpretation about the details of the return of the Lord Jesus Christ to this earth.

Gradually the latter half of the twentieth century has seen a recovery by evangelicals of a commitment to the demonstration of the love of Christ in deeds as well as words. This is not a new conviction, it simply marks a homecoming for evangelicals, as many of their forerunners in the eighteenth and nineteenth centuries saw the preaching of the Gospel and its visible embodiment through acts of mercy as being inseparably linked.

What began this recovery was a reassertion of biblical moral values. But it has not stopped there. They have recognised that the God of the Bible is concerned with all the affairs of humankind. the conviction has grown that a commitment to moral issues must similarly involve a practical response to matters of social concern such as poverty and homelessness. Anguish over an individual's moral welfare can never exclude a passion to reverse social injustice and inequality. Far from being separate options these two concerns represent two sides of the same coin!

(d) *American* – Closely allied to the moralistic impression is the view that evangelicalism is an American export to the United Kingdom.

Because fundamentalists are more numerous in the United States, and the influence (generally very positive and supportive) of high-profile American-based evangelists like Billy Graham was clearly visible on evangelicals in the UK, parallels were drawn with the American situation. The suspicion has grown in the popular press that evangelicals are merely a British 'moral-majority' movement. The well-publicised fact that the majority of American evangelicals vote for the Republican party resulted in the idea that all evangelicals vote Conservative. A right-wing, moralising group devoid of a social conscience became the unavoidable caricature of evangelicalism in the United Kingdom.

Here again the perception belies the reality of the situation. It is true that the overwhelming majority of evangelical Christians are pro-life and anti-pornography. Pro-abortion and euthanasia lobbies, coupled with the perceived collapse of marital fidelity and family values are causes of genuine concern. Yet the recognition by evangelicals of their social conscience has resulted in practical caring concern which clearly indicates that a passion for social justice and moral conviction can co-exist happily. Evangelical parachurch societies provide good models of practical action in areas of homelessness, care for the elderly and the support of single parents. Many local churches have developed important community involvement programmes, including mother and toddler groups, care for the bereaved and job creation training for the unemployed. In the case of those suffering from Aids this co-existence can be clearly seen. For while evangelicals have taken a clear stand against homosexual practice and heterosexual promiscuity they have cared for Aids sufferers and their families.

It is this combination of moral and social activism that proves to be so confusing for observers. Kenneth Clarke once remarked on his surprise, as a Government minister, that one moment I would be representing moral issues to him and the next addressing an area of social concern. His subsequent question was illuminating, 'What are you evangelicals, are you left wing or right?' My reply was that we are both!

For evangelicals in the United Kingdom provide an interesting variety of political perspectives. There is no homogeneity of allegiance, either among voters or the politicians themselves. One recent survey has suggested that while the overwhelming majority of evangelicals over 55 vote Conservative, of those in their thirties and forties the majority are Liberal Democrats. Furthermore, among those under 35 the percentage who vote Labour is higher than those of other age-groups.

This diversity would not perhaps be paralleled in the USA. Yet Anglo-American relations between evangelicals are strong, and increasingly North Americans are learning to appreciate the cultural differences and strengths which exist on both sides of the Atlantic.

(e) *Dogmatism* – evangelicals have frequently been indicted for the simplistic nature of their faith and for bigotry. Richard Holloway, the Anglican Bishop of Edinburgh, has accused evangelicals of an inability to think in complex terms and a consistent desire to adopt simple explanations and theories. He maintains that the evangelical student movement displays an 'adolescent arrogance and intemperateness'.[6] When this same bishop was widely reported as suggesting that human promiscuity was genetic in origin I was forced to reply in a TV newscast that he was over-simplifying the human condition. If we possess a 'promiscuity gene' then might we not also have a genetic excuse for acts of child-abuse, rape, or even murder. Oversimplification does not appear to be a solely evangelical trait.

The development of evangelical theological scholarship in recent years would suggest to many that they have outgrown this condition. Once it might have been simply asserted that, 'Scripture says' and therefore it must be believed. Contemporary evangelicalism will not deny biblical authority, but will frequently take the opportunity of further explaining the grounds on which Scripture makes its claims, and why these should be accepted.

If we are to believe our critics then evangelicals may well be regarded as those who have rejected human reason and fallen for a glib, moralistic triumphalism. The simple fact remains that the detractors of evangelicalism may not be wholly correct in their accusations. They may well be accurate when applied to special individuals, churches or isolated incidents. However, to generalise and indict *all* evangelicals on these charges could constitute a major miscarriage of justice.

Evangelicalism is not static, it is in a state of flux, and many would argue that while these accusations contain a germ of truth, there is often a different side to the story!

The problem remains that many evangelicals have accepted these criticisms, and come at least to partially believe them. Some would maintain that they are now post-evangelicals, others would hesitate to accept an evangelical identity for fear of implying an acceptance of values that are believed to accompany it!

Recovering our identity

'I suppose you would have to simply describe me as an evangelical.' The confession was dragged out of me. Others were calling themselves 'liberal', 'catholic', 'eclectic' or 'middle-of-the-road'. Everyone was seeking to define their theological position by a simple phrase, and I had no alternative other than to adopt the single word that most clearly identified what I believed.

I have to admit that this would not always have been the case. As a young evangelist I encountered a critical question from a young Free Church pastor in a larger gathering of clergy. My response was to announce, 'But I wouldn't call myself that. No, I'm not an evangelical.' That phrase typified a trendy assumption of the 1970s. The word 'evangelical' carried with it some cultural baggage that I was not prepared to accept. It smacked of doctrinal smugness, resistance to change, and reluctance to become involved in the socio-political issues that afflicted society. I saw evangelicals as those who tried to hide away from the real world. My reaction was intended to demonstrate how open I was to dialogue with the many non-evangelicals at that meeting – but it was also a lie. For I had received my theological training at an evangelical college, and still remained convinced that the doctrines I had learned there were the right ones! I had been converted at 19 and knew what it was to be forgiven for the way I had lived. I spent my time preaching Jesus, and I trusted Scripture and was firmly committed to biblical doctrine. The problem was simple. I was evangelical, I just resented being identified as one. There was too much in contemporary evangelicalism that I just did not like.

The pastor was horrified. He felt that I was denying the reality of all I claimed to stand for. He could recognise that I had become confused by the 'spirit of the age' towards evangelicalism. I was rejecting the truth that I acknowledged because of confusion over all the connotations that I understood were now associated with that one word.

The vehemence of his reaction surprised me, but it made me think. I would have preferred to call myself a 'charismatic', but while that said something about my experience of God, it failed to represent my overall doctrinal position. I believed in Jesus, his miracles and bodily resurrection, I trusted the authority of Scripture, I recognised human sin and the need for a Saviour. Yet human vocabulary and prejudice had undermined my basic position, it took two years before I could freely acknowledge my identity as an evangelical Christian. Sadly, that young pastor died before I could tell him that his words that night had successfully nagged away at me through ensuing months. He first made me see that issues I had deemed irrelevant were vital, and that truth is more important than popularity.

In the years that have followed I have become increasingly convinced that we need to know who we are as evangelicals, and to recognise what distinguishes us as such. I have also had to recognise the reluctance that Christians have to adopt labels for themselves.

In the light of all that has been said in the last chapter about unity within the church such a reaction would appear to be perfectly logical. Many still sympathise with the lady who, at the conclusion of a church service, expressed her frustration to a visiting preacher. She demanded to know, 'Why do we need labels? Can't we just call ourselves Christians?'

If the word 'evangelical' has previously generated misunder-standing and confusion, the same principle applies even more to the term 'Christian'. So many assumptions are readily made:

– living in a Christian country make you a Christian
– being baptised as an infant makes you a Christian
– going to church makes you a Christian
– doing good to your neighbour makes you a Christian.

One friend was conducting a school lesson and on asking the simple question 'What is a Christian?' received the illuminating reply that a Christian was someone who grew their own vegetables!

Such confusion is not always humorous. On one occasion a BBC news report referred to a car bomb which had exploded in the centre of the civilian population of Beirut. The reporter explained that this latest atrocity was the work of the 'Christian Militia' – yet any listener with a minimum understanding of the Christian faith would surely realise that a savage act of murder is a million miles removed from the character of the man from Nazareth who taught that people should love their enemies.

The word 'Christian' therefore itself requires some explanation. Churchgoers themselves can be divided into different traditions – Catholic, Orthodox, liberal, broad church and evangelical each adopt their own perspectives. While Catholics and the Orthodox emphasise the significance of tradition, the broad church the importance of tolerance, liberals the necessity to employ human reason, evangelicals maintain the prime authority of Scripture. While each tradition believes in Jesus, their understanding of Christian belief and practice will be conditioned by these funda-mental presuppositions.

The distinguishing features of evangelicals have always included an insistence on four priorities:

- The supreme authority of Scripture.
- The uniqueness of redemption through Christ's death.
- The need for personal conversion.
- The urgent necessity for evangelism.[7]

Alongside these some have added the Lordship of the Holy Spirit and the divine and majestic character of Jesus Christ.[8] To these fundamental priorities all evangelicals will give their assent. On other issues they may well endure internal disagreements, but over these primary matters evangelical Christians cannot and will not compromise.

While it is hard to arrive at a precise definition of evangelicalism John Stott has emphasised that the two major hallmarks of evangelicals are that they are Bible people and gospel people.[9] He insists that, 'the evangelical faith is not some eccentric deviation from historic Christianity. On the contrary, in our conviction it is Christianity in its purest and most primitive form'.[10]

The sugggestion has been made that evangelicalism is really a subculture, in that it is more concerned with behaviour patterns than specific doctrines.[11] This argument may well be supported by evangelical attitudes at certain periods in history. During the 1950s and 1960s evangelicals tended to add to the fundamental truths of the gospel certain legalistic taboos of conduct. Most evangelicals accepted prohibitions on cinema, alcohol, dancing, smoking and going to the theatre. These attitudes largely depended on cultural background.

I remember attending a large international evangelical conference in Brazil. The host nation was exceptionally proud of the fact that one of the conference staff had won the Miss Brazil beauty contest in the previous year. On one specific night this delightful girl was invited to give her testimony. As she stood up to do so the Dutch delegation walked out in protest. They felt that a competitor for the Miss World title, involved in the 'beauty business', was an inappropriate contributor to an evangelical conference. At the end of the evening, as the other delegates left the conference hall, the Dutch delegates were sitting at the bar drinking beer and smoking cigars – to the surprise of their Brazilian hosts! So many of the additional requirements of evangelicalism owe at least some reference to cultural considerations – and will therefore vary with generations and geography.

At their roots evangelicals are activists committed to a personal relationship with Christ, but acknowledging that at all times this relationship and their activism must always be consistent with the teaching of Scripture. For this reason inconsistencies will emerge, for evangelicals will often interpret Scripture differently from each other.

It is precisely because evangelicalism is primarily about truths to be believed that here the major tensions occur. For the tendency emerges to add secondary matters to primary evangelical doctrines. Today these may focus around the individual's experience of the Holy Spirit, our response to the debate between theistic evolution and creation science, or our attitude towards ecumenism. All these issues are important in their own right, but they have not previously been regarded as arbiters of evangelical orthodoxy.

If theological and cultural considerations of this kind are given too much prominence hopes of evangelical unity will soon evaporate. Past decades have seen evangelicals racked by dissension over issues of church order, the sacraments, predestination and Christian ministry. Each generation produces their own areas of tension. The danger comes when these assume prominence in our thinking and take precedence above our concern for evangelical unity.

It has been wisely pointed out that matters which unite evangelicals are far greater than those which divide us. We share the conviction that Scripture is a trustworthy record of God's revelation of himself to humankind. We agree together that through his death on the cross Christ brings those who surrender their lives to him in repentance and faith into a personal relationship with the Creator God. These truths are vital to us. We can also freely concede that evangelicals do not have a total monopoly over these truths. There will be those in Orthodox and Catholic traditions who believe as we do, but choose to worship in a different fashion. Others in a liberal position may well be on a journey to faith. It is not for us to maintain exclusiveness of position which is reflected in a refusal to learn from others, and an arrogant condemnation of their own position.

Some have suggested that to call ourselves 'evangelical Christians' is, in itself, divisive. The word 'evangelical' is sometimes thought to still convey too many misconceptions. Yet, as Dr Derek Tidball, the Principal of London Bible College, has wisely observed, 'There is something distinctive about evangelicalism. Abandoning the word would be like abandoning spectacles and would prevent us from bringing contemporary Christianity into any kind of focus.'[12]

It is quite possible to maintain a position in which we disagree with others, without being obnoxious in doing so. As evangelicals we can raise an argument that Catholicism is evangelical faith with tradition added to it, therefore distorting its true focus. We can suggest that liberalism is evangelicalism minus its conviction of biblical authority and revealed truth, therefore removing the basis of our faith.

These statements may sound harsh – but not unnecessarily so. They can be conveyed in a thoughtful, irenic manner, as can non-evangelical criticisms of evangelicals as narrow in their vision and rigid in their judgements. Such statements can be the focus of helpful debate rather than bitter division.

For this to emerge evangelicals have first to recover their own sense of history and identity. We need to know who we are, and how to respond to our critics. We need to be less sensitive about the fact that we do possess opinions and beliefs. We need to be unashamed of being evangelicals.

For many years I have challenged congregations to recognise that 'an evangelical is someone who believes that the Bible is the Word of God; that Jesus is the Son of God; who holds to the traditional credal statements of the Church and owns a commitment to Jesus Christ as their Saviour, Lord and King'. If that statement includes you and you accept my definition, then I suggest that makes you an evangelical. Now all we have to do is live up to its true heritage, character and meaning!

3

'Blest be the tie that binds'

The Nature of our Unity

Many will be familiar with the name of the highly-accomplished hymn writer, Graham Kendrick. They will have sung many of his songs, and appreciated his ministry. Yet few will be aware of what Graham was referring to when he wrote these words:

> Becoming part of a team ministry has been a priceless experience. It has often proved painful too, but then the love of Christ came not without pain for it led him to the cross. Taking his example we have had to begin to learn how to share ourselves, to love one another, to walk 'in the light' together, that in the words of Jesus, 'By this will all men know that you are my disciples, if you have love one for another.'[1]

Those words, written over twenty years ago, retain intense poignancy for me. Graham, my wife Ruth and I were involved together in a team called 'In the Name of Jesus'. Ten of us began together on 10 July 1973, and for each of us it was to prove a life changing experience.

When you are suddenly thrown together with nine other people problems are inevitable! We had to learn to appreciate the differences in each personality, to draw out the talents of one another, and to love each other under the intense pressure of church and college-based missions. We needed to be honest, sincere and committed in our relationships, learning how to both relax and work together. Instead of being able to hide behind our words we had to go into local churches and live out the message we had been given. None of us was over 25 years of age. Inevitably we were all fairly immature and made far too many mistakes, but God is gracious, and never over-concerned with the quality of people he is only just beginning to mould. We discovered that, for the three years we were together, God spoke through our friendship and relationship as much as from our words. By the end, we were not 'super-Christians' but we had learned more of Jesus, and most of that we had gained from each other.

Now life in a close-knit team is not the same as in a local church, but it did encapsulate in microcosm many of the pressures and problems of church relationships into a very short period of time. From this experience I have become convinced that there has to be more to our unity than the mutual attendance of meetings! The sober fact is that, with outstanding exceptions, many of our churches have reflected more of the externals of worship than the intimacy of personal friendship. Too many people in our congregations can feel like supportive spectators. They lack the obvious involvement of those who have immersed themselves in the life and work of the local church. This is often the real key to feeling part of the Christian community – but it reduces the church to a people who *do*, not a people who *are*. *Doing* not *being* has become the means of entry into 'the club', therefore frequently excluding those who face major family responsibilities or whose secular work demands too much of their time.

This emphasis occurs in much initial instruction to new converts. We confidently announce that now they have become Christians Jesus comes to live in their lives to bring forgiveness from sin and to introduce his new lifestyle through the Holy Spirit. We firmly explain the necessity for positive Christian behaviour – morally, financially, etc. We boldly encourage a disciplined prayer life, time spent with God in the study of Scripture, and loyal participation in the local church or fellowship. We often fail to explain that while conversion is personal the Christian life is communal. No one has to struggle to make it alone any more, we now have each other.

Too many Christians know what it is to feel isolated and alone. This was never the intention of Jesus. For being an individual Christian is only a very small part of the picture. From the moment we entrust our lives into his hands he makes us part of the family!

Those we mix and mingle with at Christian meetings are not colleagues, or fellow-members, but brothers and sisters. For we share the same Heavenly Father. It was part of our legacy from the resurrection of Jesus. Only after this event could he instruct many to, 'Go instead to my brothers and tell them' (John 20:17). Through his death he had taken his friends and made them family. This same status he conferred on all who would believe through their message (John 17:20-4) – and that includes us!

As brothers and sisters our relationship is enforced, we might not have chosen each other, we might find each other difficult, but we are 'lumbered' with each other. Our only way forward is to learn how to understand, encourage and support each other in a manner which truly reflects our obedience to what Jesus has already demanded from us.

The story is told of the apostle John, living as an elderly man in Ephesus. Transportation was provided for him by means of a stretcher on which he was carried by two of the younger (and stronger) Christians. As he passed through the marketplace John would spot groups of Christians, and he would continually call out, 'Little children, love one another'. Slightly embarrassed at this frequent interjection, those carrying him enquired as to why he spoke out in this fashion. They wondered if it was the effect of the sun, or just the meanderings of old age. The apostle's reply was succinct – 'Because the Master commanded it, and because this is the first foundation on which all else is built.'

This theme of love infects John's epistles. For how can we claim to love God if we do not love our brothers and sisters (1 John 3:10, 4:20-1). This love is not limited to words but must be demonstrated by our actions (1 John 3:18). He echoes the words of Jesus insisting on the fact that we must love each other (John 13:34-5; 1 John 3:11,23; 4:7,11; 2 John v.5).

The true nature of our unity lies in that single word, 'love'. It has often been observed that while you can choose your friends you cannot select your family. That is also true in the family of God where we are all *adelphoi* – 'brothers' – together (Matthew 18:15; 1 Corinthians 8:13; 1 John 2:10, 4:21). For Christianity is a faith that unites all true believers and the bond between us is one of love.

As Michael Green has aptly observed, 'The Christian faith is so different from all self-improvement cults and the faiths that seek fulfilment or enlightenment "for myself alone". It is inescapably corporate.'[2]

These words contradict our contemporary individualism and demand that we live sacrificial lives giving ourselves in the service of others. The fact is underlined when we consider how the New Testament writers emphasised our mutual responsibility. They did this by using the phrase 'one another' in a catalogue of expectations that God places upon his people.

- Romans 12:10a – 'Be devoted to one another'; 12:10b – 'Honour one another'; 12:16 – 'Live in harmony with one another'; 15:7 –'Accept one another'.
- 1Corinthians 12:25 – Express 'equal concern for each other'.
- Galatians 5:13 – 'Serve one another in love'; 6:2 – 'Carry each other's burdens'.
- Ephesians 4:32 – 'Be kind and compassionate to one another, forgiving each other . . .'; 5:19 – 'Speak to one another with psalms, hymns and spiritual songs'; 5:21 – 'Submit to one another'.
- Philippians 2:4 – 'Look . . . to the interests of others'.
- Colossians 3:13a – 'Bear with each other'; 3:13b – 'Forgive whatever grievances you may have against one another'; 3:16 – 'Admonish one another'.
- 1Thessalonians 3:12 – 'May the Lord make your love increase and overflow for each other'; 4:18 – 'Encourage each other'.
- Hebrews 3:13, 10:25 – 'Encourage one another'; 10:24 – 'Spur one another on towards love and good deeds'.
- James 4:11 – 'Do not slander one another'; 5:16a – 'Confess your sins to each other'; 5:16b – 'Pray for each other'.
- 1Peter 4:8 – 'Love each other deeply'; 4:9 – 'Offer hospitality to one another without grumbling'; 5:5 – 'Clothe yourselves with humility toward one another'.

A privatised view of faith is therefore an unbiblical perspective. It is incompatible with the clear teaching of Scripture. For love is the key that brings us together in a shared relationship of mutual concern as children of the living God. But the question remains – how do we do it? We understand the commands given to us but how can we fulfil them? By what means is this love to be experienced and expressed?

(i) Partnership

The old hymn speaks glowingly of that which unites us together in partnership, 'Blest be the tie that binds/Our hearts in Christian love'.[3] To uncover what the 'tie' actually is we have to turn to the pages of the New Testament, and more specifically to the Greek text. There we frequently encounter the word *koinonia*, and its root meaning is 'partnership' or 'fellowship'.

The mere mention of a word like 'fellowship' is liable to provoke extremes of reaction among believers. Like the church notice board that announced a 'revival meeting' on Thursday evening, a 'fellowship' evening can represent a statement of hope rather than prophetic certainty. Such times can be important in helping to create a sense of 'belonging', but to term them *koinonia* trivialises the word. The heartbeat of evangelical unity must lie in more than a meeting. To view it as merely our physical presence in the same room is to evacuate much of the meaning from a concept central to our relationship with each other as fragmented parts of the one Body of Christ.

The Greek noun *koinonia*, and the adjectives and verbs associated with it, occur no less than 45 times in the New Testament. The word is usually translated as 'communion' or 'fellowship', yet it had been borrowed from everyday life in New Testament times. In secular society it was used to describe friendship and co-operation in business, sports and personal relationships. Among the Greek philosophers it was something to be pursued, an ideal of brotherly love and co-operation. This word was used by the early Christian writers to express the quality of relationships required within the local church. It is employed three times by Luke, seven by John, once by Matthew, three by Peter, three by the author of the epistle of the Hebrews, and no less than 28 times by Paul. It is therefore a significant term for our Christian unity.

Koinonia implies far more than unity in terms of a common faith or shared membership in a single institution. It can never be reduced to a concept of 'fellowship' which means little more than a sense of bonhomie among believers! For this only devalues its rich meaning. True *koinonia* means far more. In both classical and

New Testament Greek its primary focus is not simply an association with others, but refers to our joint participation in something which we share together.[4] In other words it means 'a personal relationship, or partnership, based on mutual commitment to each other and to a common purpose, often springing from the fact that both parties already participate in something together'.[5]

The predominant idea in the New Testament is of:

(a) Having a share (Philippians 1:7; 1Peter 5:1; 2Peter 1:4).
(b) Giving a share (Romans 15:26; 2Corinthians 9:13; Philippians 1:5).
(c) Sharing (Acts 2:42; Gal 2:9).

The concept is therefore one of partnership. This idea does not relate to our contemporary idea of a partner as a sexual mate but denotes a close personal relationship with others who are also 'in Christ'. Our partnership is not based on what we do but in whom we share.

We do not share together in sin or false teaching (1Corinthians 10:20; 1Timothy 5:22; 2John 11; Revelation 18:4), but are in partnership with God himself – Father, Son and Holy Spirit (1Corinthians 1:9; 2Corinthians 13:14; Philippians 2:1; 1John 1:3,6). This sense of 'oneness' in Jesus Christ stems from our *koinonia* together and represents alone the foundation stone for all true biblical unity.

Such partnership can overcome all barriers presented by racial or social divisions. This was witnessed by the church in Antioch. A black man (Simeon called 'niger') an ex-Sanhedrin member (Saul of Tarsus), a wealthy Cypriot (Barnabas), a member of the Judean royalty (King Herod's foster brother Manaea), and presumably the usual sprinkling of slaves all met as one body in Christ. They shared the leadership together. Here Jews and Gentiles discovered a partnership in Jesus which overcame all the anti-Semitism and anti-gentilism of the centuries because they were one in the Spirit of God.

It was at Antioch that *koinonia* partnership could be seen in action. 'The man at the very peak of the social pile and the man at the bottom met together in the church of the Lord Jesus Christ and they were one in a beauty of relationships.'[6]

(ii) Honesty

It often seems that our ingrained sense of British reserve can act as a major barrier to true partnership. We remain too afraid of rejection to allow our brothers and sisters to see who we really are. This can lead to the careful cultivation of counterfeit spirituality designed to portray what we would like to be rather than the lesser reality of our current condition. We can hide behind the mask of a plastic grin, smiling to disguise the real hurt that we feel inside, trying to hide away from view the genuine 'me'.

Sunday by Sunday thousands leave our churches and fellowships to receive the customary handshake and friendly enquiry from the minister, vicar, elder or pastor. One could reconstruct the normal conversation in the following manner, but adding in brackets the thoughts that lie behind the words that are uttered:

'How are you?'

'I'm fine' (I feel lousy really!)

'How's the wife?'

'She's fine' (but today I can't imagine why on earth I married her).

'How are the children?'

'They're fine' (they are also the reason that the wife's in such a state, scream, scream, scream, especially the little one).

'And how's your job?'

'Fine.' (You stupid . . . don't you know about the redundancies – me included!)

'And how's your spiritual life?'

'Fine.' (Well, with that lot going on what do you think it's like?)[7]

Such dishonesty is not confined to the members of congregations. Nor is it limited to larger churches and fellowships. Some years ago a married couple who I know well faced similar enquiries at the door of their South Coast Baptist church. The wife was more honest than her husband and replied, 'It's really dreadful, we just do not know what to do'. The minister's response was not typical for all he could say was, 'Fine, good evening'. The tragedy was that his pastoral skills could not cope with such blunt honesty.

Behind such extremes lies a spark of truth for each one of us. Fearing rejection we are often reluctant to expose ourselves to each other. Yet God never intended that we should struggle with our problems alone, for true *koinonia* means that we can share each other's hurts and needs.

Whether our problems are economic, emotional, sexual, racial or psychological the church was designed to be a supportive community of which we are a part. For help to be given requires openness on our part, and trustworthiness from those with whom we share. It is in genuine communication, as we become vulnerable to one another, that reliable friends can give us the counsel and support that we need (2Corinthians 6:11).

It is a liberating experience to discover that others can love and accept us for what we are, not the person that we might have pretended to be. Then we can move on together in our spiritual lives, because 'walking in the light' with each other has proved to be the doorway to genuine fellowship (1John 1:7).

(iii) Encouragement
We live in a society which continually urges us towards self-improvement and self-promotion. In contrast the Bible encourages us to promote the needs and achievements of others. By this means we can actively demonstrate an alternative lifestyle. Instead of being totally caught up in ourselves we become committed to the support of one another. In adopting this attitude we comply with the words of Jesus when he said, 'It is more blessed to give than receive' (Acts 20:35).

One vivid biblical example of this principle is found in a man named Joseph. He was so committed to the support of others that he was nicknamed Barnabas, which simply meant 'son of encouragement' (Acts 4:36). When Paul was regarded by the disciples as unfit material for Jesus to work on, Barnabas believed in him and testified to others as to the genuineness of his conversion (Acts 9:27). He took Paul to Antioch, and went on a missionary journey with him, even being prepared to take second place in the partnership (Acts 11:25, 13:42).

It was Barnabas who saw the potential in John Mark, forgave his failure, and even parted with Paul when John Mark was rejected for their next proposed journey together. Barnabas persisted with John Mark and they travelled back to Cyprus to continue the work there (Acts 15:36-9).

It is significant to note that Paul wrote up to thirteen epistles, and Mark contributed a gospel, Barnabas never wrote a book contained in the canon of the New Testament. Yet without his gift of encouragement to Paul and Mark we might not have, in present form, one half of the books of the New Testament! This same gift of encouragement should exist among us today. It will be there as we exhibit emotional support, standing with each other and sharing in the pain and joys of our brothers and sisters (Romans 12:15).

Equally we will be involved in giving nurture and counsel to those who require it, taking an active interest in the spiritual survival and growth of one another, as well as ourselves (Ephesians 5:10; Colossians 3:16). For the challenge we face is to live as an organism not an organisation. Just as the eye cannot fulfil the functions of an ear, or vice versa, so we too need each other (1 Corinthians 12:25).

Nowhere is our commitment to mutual support meant to become more obvious than in the area of solid practical help for one another. In everyday terms this means that if another Christian is desperately short of resources, and we have more than we need, then it should be shared. The same principle applies to the car in the garage, the spare bed, the empty seat at the meal table, or the gifts and skills that we have been given or acquired. If the bereaved in the community received friendship, the unemployed were given job training, the elderly were visited, the disabled had their shopping done and the single parent invited to join an extended family – would society not sit up and take notice? Christian fellowship was never intended to be just a matter of theory, it is there to be practised in order that we might give visible support and encouragement to each other.

One speaker at the annual Spring Harvest festival returned home with her family after three weeks at the event. A few days later, she was at the informal regular meeting of wives from the local church. She shared with them her despair at the number of domestic tasks she had to face on returning home. Three weeks of family washing and ironing, the house to clean, the shopping to do, all alongside her responsibilities in the church and the local community. In an unguarded moment she wistfully commented, 'If only I had come home to find that someone had cut the grass'.

Immediately she received a sharp rebuke. 'Who do you think

you are? None of us has our lawn mown when we're away enjoying ourselves on holiday.'

The comment is perhaps natural enough. But the Spring Harvest speaker could be forgiven for thinking that giving out spiritually for a minimum of twelve hours a day, over three weeks, had scarcely been a holiday! Didn't someone once speak of 'bearing one another's burdens'? And if the grass had been cut, would the neighbours not have seen a quality of church life that they might have missed before?[8] For *koinonia* must be worked out in practice, and encouragement given a tangible quality that is demonstrably obvious to all who are prepared to notice it.

Perhaps the most important area of all is the need to speak words of encouragement to one another. For our speech can bring either healing or pain. Gossip, criticism, jealousy, quarrelling and backbiting are all destructive vices, and there is an alternative! Instead of stabbing each other in the back, and wounding the body of Christ, we can encourage one another. By this means we spur fellow Christians on to love and good deeds (Hebrews 10:24–5). We strengthen and build each other up (1 Thessalonians 3:2, 5:11; 2 Thessalonians 2:16–17). This, in turn, reinforces our sense of community and provides refreshment and deeper unity for God's people (Romans 15:5; 1 Thessalonians 4:18, 5:14; Philemon v7; Hebrews 10:25).

Where older Christians encourage their younger counterparts the generation barrier is broken down. Through prayerful concern, speaking up for those who are being criticised, and seeking to mentor those younger in the faith, we re-introduce the 'Barnabas factor' into our church lives today. This lies at the heart of *koinonia*, and many look back with affection and respect on those who first encouraged them in this kind of way.

For myself, I first encountered the international evangelist Luis Palau at Spring Harvest in 1979. He swiftly identified me as a brash but enthusiastic young man – who needed help! When Luis discovered that no one had 'taken me under their wing' he invited me to travel with him in the United States for a few weeks in 1980.

I made the grave mistake of assuming that I would only be carrying his bags. This turned out to be far from true. Time after time Luis would pause in mid-sermon and ask me to take over for a few minutes. He introduced me to church and denominational leaders, took me to meet diplomats and ambassadors, gave me the first experience of a television broadcast, and even provided a seat at a Presidential press conference. The experience was fantastic, and his trust in me an enormous encouragement. Three years later I was appointed as general secretary of the Evangelical Alliance UK. The foresight Luis showed, the preparation he provided, and the encouragement he and his wife Pat gave will never be forgotten. That, for me, was *koinonia* in action.

The kind of leadership we will receive in the church tomorrow may largely depend on our willingness to follow his example today in preparing a new generation of younger leaders who will be ready for their future ministry.

(iv) Commitment

The New Testament teaches both clearly and unequivocally that Jesus came into this world to redeem, not merely a number of individuals in isolation, but a people for himself. He insisted that he would build his Church and Paul wrote that his purpose was 'to purify for himself a people that are His very own' (Tit 2:14). Therefore we can affirm that, 'he not only died for *me* and gave himself for *me*, but also for *us*, for me in company with all the other saved people or believers in him – a Church, *the* Church, *his* Church, the Church of the Living God. God's declared purpose has always been to redeem a whole great company of people into fellowship with himself, and with one another in him.'[9] For this reason it is not enough to be committed to Jesus, submission to his revealed will means that we will also become committed to one another.

This kind of commitment to one another was exhibited in biblical friendships. It existed between Ruth and Naomi (Ruth 1:16), David and Jonathan (1 Samuel 20:17), and Elijah and Elisha (2 Kings 2:2). These were friendships that were not casual or superficial, their commitment together meant that they did not give up on each other. This consistency in relationships together was denoted by the great Hebrew word *hesedh*, which means 'covenant love' (Proverbs 17:17).

Jesus called those who obeyed him, his friends (John 15:14–15). This friendship should be the hallmark of our unity. It is not enough to regard ourselves as Christian colleagues. We are all friends of each other – because we share the friendship of Jesus.

This sounds easy in theory, but working it out in practice can be another matter entirely! I will never forget preaching one evening on the subject of unity. At the conclusion of the evening a young married woman was still seated, and crying bitterly. I went up to her, adopting my best pastoral manner (such as it is), and putting my arm around her asked what the trouble was? 'I don't know how to say this – but I just don't like you,' was the stark reply. Now it's fine to talk about a subject in the abstract, but I was shattered to gain a crash course in first-hand experience. It was all that I could do to keep my arm around her and pray that God who is the author of love would teach us a loving acceptance and respect for each other.

Many of us do acquire what can become long-standing problems with our fellow Christians. God has created us all so different in character that we will not automatically relate positively to everyone else. But Jesus does command us to love each other, and his instruction is not given without the offer of the grace and strength to carry it out.

It is as we commit ourselves together to live in friendship we begin to emulate the life of the church as it was always designed to be lived. In Acts and the epistles we see infant churches emerging as practising communities in which individuals discovered a corporate life as they learned to support one another. Their fellowship did not lie in merely attending meetings together, it had its roots in something that was far deeper. They freely shared material possessions, met the spiritual and physical needs of each other, and provided prayer and encouragement for all the Christian family. They practised a mutual friendship which extended to all aspects of life and lifestyle. From that foundation their corporate prayer, ministry and activities came together because these were grounded in fellowship. This fellowship was, in reality, a 'worshipping friendship'.

(v) Forgiveness

Friendship of this kind must never be artificial, it must have its roots in reality. Here 'the rubber hits the road', for so many of us find it incredibly difficult to get on with each other.

Within secular society we can simply choose to avoid those whose personality, attitudes or perspectives are not those to which we would naturally warm. This is not a luxury that we are permitted in the life of the Church. For we are to forgive those who have wronged us, love those who hate and abuse us, and esteem others as being better than ourselves (Romans 12:10, Philippians 2:3). That much-misquoted passage in Matthew's gospel does not insist that we should only forgive our brother before taking our gift to God, it demands that we should first seek reconciliation with those who have something against us (Matthew 5:23–4).

Some relationships will be harder to form than others, some will just fall into place, and others will take months of working out. It is often those relationships which have to be worked at, between those of opposite character, that eventually prove to be the deepest and most profitable. We must not excuse ourselves by saying that we don't get on with someone else. If both parties want to, and open themselves to God's direction, he comes to help us overcome our mutual antipathy.

It has been wisely observed that, 'If you have problems with people – you have problems'. The Holy Spirit is not unaware of our needs in this area, he comes to help us develop tolerance and mutual understanding, to build bridges towards one another, and to meet each other at our point of need. After all, he is the only one who can provide spiritual unity and the grace and strength to carry it out.

I will never forget the moment that Graham Kendrick had to say to me, 'Clive, I just don't trust you. Your mind works too fast, you're always planning two steps ahead, there are so many ideas and schemes running around – but I do trust God in you.' That is one aspect of real forgiveness – not just for wrongs committed, but for the defects in our attitudes and personalities. The fact is that our lives impinge directly on each other, sometimes the unconscious damage that we can inflict by threatening or manipulating others is more devastating than our conscious direct action. There is also the capacity for understanding that none of us is perfect. We all make mistakes, and have on occasions done completely the wrong thing. But God is at work in us! He does not leave us in isolation, but is working to refine our lives! Each of us needs to recognise this in one another, hoping that the day will soon dawn when friends are as fault-free as ourselves!

This is why we must never justify breaking off relationships with a brother or sister because of a particular incident which takes place. Too often it is an accident or a mistake, and forgiveness is necessary. No Christian – be they preacher, evangelist, housewife or student is infallible – we all endure off-days, and we all make mistakes. Forgiveness is part of the package of Christian friendship and we should all be prepared to make the first move in seeking to restore damaged relationships.

Jesus taught his disciples to pray that God would forgive them in the same way that they forgave others (Matthew 6:12). The clear implication was that our attitude towards forgiving others should reflect the manner in which we expect God to forgive us! As forgiven people our relationships together need to mirror our relationship with Jesus Christ. Attitudes of resentment, bitterness and alienation must have no place in our lives, they need to be replaced by an ongoing desire for reconciliation and restored relationships.

This was the clear expectation and teaching of Jesus reflected supremely in his example of sacrificial love demonstrated on the cross (Luke 23:34). He instructed his followers to love their enemies (Matthew 5:44), to forgive on 'seventy-seven times' occasions (Matthew 18:22), and to leave revenge in his hands not our own (Romans 12:19). We are left with only one option, that of forgiveness. We forgive others for the simple reason that Christ has forgiven us for all our sins (Ephesians 4:32; Colossians 3:13). However, we are not only left with strong reasons to offer forgiveness. We are also given the power of the Holy Spirit to forgive that which we might assume to be unforgivable. That is the heart of the Christian grace that God wants to work out in and through our lives.

This will apply even where we may think that we have been 'right'. For we are to speak the truth and confront each other in our areas of disagreement, but such truth must always be spoken 'in love' (Ephesians 4:15). We have always to remember that we are communicating with individuals who may be delicate and insecure, but each one is precious in God's sight. The cold harsh voice of arrogant orthodoxy has never been a blessing to anyone.

Even if we are correct in what we say we can put ourselves in the wrong by our own feelings of pride and injustice. Our 'rightness' is measured by the way in which we are 'completely humble and gentle; ... patient, bearing with one another in love' (Ephesians 4:2).

We possess no God-given prerogative to judge and correct others, this is a privilege we earn by our loving commitment to them. It is never adequate to say to someone, 'Look, I want to put you right. You hurt me the other day. What you did was stupid and wrong. I thought you needed to be aware of the damage you have done.' Instead we must emulate Paul's attitude of love (see 1Corinthians 13:3–4). Such an attitude freely concedes, 'I'm sorry, I misunderstood you and have become bitter and resentful. Could we pray together?' Such a confession should always be followed by prayer that God will remove hurt and condemnation from both parties – and restore the relationship. Even if we are rejected we will have acted in a Godly fashion. As A. W. Tozer put it. 'Always it is more important that we retain a right spirit towards others, than that we bring them to our way of thinking, even if our way is right.'[10]

This then is true forgiveness, and genuine *koinonia* fellowship. It models itself on the servant-heart of Jesus who looked, not to his own reputation, but to the needs of others (Philippians 2:6–8). This attitude of servanthood means that we share our joys and sorrows together (1Corinthians 12:26–7), and act as the servant, not the ruler, of others (Mark 9:35, 10:44). Perhaps the greatest demonstration of all came when Jesus adopted the lowest position in the household in order to wash his disciples' filthy feet (John 13:4–5). It is this self-evaluation, that looks to the interests of others not our own, which lies at the heart of the Christian distinctive that can most impress secular society – we love each other. That is the ground of our unity. It is what Jesus requires from each of his followers.

4

All one in Christ

It is not easy to write a book on evangelical unity! For we live in a society where tolerance has become the most important virtue and convinced belief is relegated to the status of a prop to support the inadequate. Our 'postmodernist' world insists that truth like beauty only exists in the eye of the beholder. Each person must develop their own concept of what is right and wrong, of religion as they perceive it, and find a lifestyle that is suitable for themselves. What must never happen is an attempt to impose our beliefs on others.

To speak of unity is therefore to cultivate a mutual acceptance of one another. We are united under 'the Fatherhood of God', within 'the brotherhood of man'. To proceed with further qualification would invite accusations of narrow-mindedness and intolerance. Unity can therefore never be reduced to any single group of people who combine on the basis of shared convictions. An understanding of our common humanity must overcome all such restrictions.

There is something terribly appealing in this viewpoint. It touches a chord within each of us. But its bias is rooted in the certainty that, as people, we are ourselves the measure of all things. If humankind is all there is of ultimate worth in the universe then our unity together is of paramount importance. Surely wars, famine and injustice would all be obliterated if we could simply release each other to 'do your own thing'?

However, a more realistic assessment suggests otherwise. Human selfishness and greed has always intervened to destroy this utopian ideal. Creation and conscience combine to suggest that we are not alone in the universe. If we cannot manufacture our own 'brave new world', then perhaps there is a God after all? If God does exist, then our unity is not just with each other, He is involved – and our understanding of unity will need to transcend mere human collaboration.

For this is an issue of fundamental importance. If God exists then he does not only unite, he also divides people. The primary division will always be between those who acknowledge, love and serve him in relationship together, and those who do not. The Bible refers to one condition as 'light' and the other as 'darkness', it affirms that light shines in the darkness, and darkness can never either understand or overcome it (John 1:4).

Jesus himself asked the question, 'Do you think I came to bring peace on earth?' His reply must have astonished his disciples. 'No, I tell you, but division. From now on there will be five in one family divided against each other, three against two and two against three. They will be divided . . .' (Luke 12:51–3). For while we are united in our common humanity, we are divided in our reaction to Jesus. Some will reject his claims on their lives, others will accept his offer of forgiveness and new life which he made from a cross. In the light of the truth of Jesus Christ our unity with those who deny his love can never be more than skin deep.

It was Easter, and therefore for myself and the family this involved three weeks away from home at the annual Spring Harvest festival which is attended by up to 80,000 Christians per annum. This year it took on a particular significance, for the Archbishop of Canterbury, Dr George Carey, had agreed to pay a special visit to the event. As the crowds settled down comfortably in the Big Top I prepared for an hour of face-to-face with the Archbishop. I enjoy his company and greatly appreciated the fact that he was prepared to be with us for that day. However, knowing that many of our speakers and guests would have questions for him, I had suggested that I might pose these to him for around an hour. He had willingly agreed, so the evening before had invited whatever questions people might wish to submit. These ranged from his choice of breakfast cereal to his attitude towards homosexual clergy. The answers were succinct and enlightening, the whole session being greeted with warm enthusiasm from those who were present.

One provocative question posed by a member of the speaker

team still sticks out in my mind: 'Archbishop – which is the more important, unity or truth?' As usual the reply was courteous and informative. Both must be maintained together. That is right, but I was tempted to ask which, in cases of total conflict, should take precedence? Can truth be sacrificed on the altar of unity, or vice versa? What is the ultimate ground for affirming that we are all one in Christ Jesus? How far may our view of truth be compromised in the interests of unity? How united are we entitled to be?

(i) In defence of the truth

It is the evangelical conviction that true unity lies with those who share a mutual understanding of truth as it is revealed in Jesus Christ.

Such oneness is not created by uniformity. We are not all the same as one another. Our intrinsic individuality will provide each one of us with specific emphases and perspectives. We must never allow ourselves to be mere clones of each other, a bunch of evangelical 'Homepride flour graders' churned out on a conveyor belt. But differences will be evident on secondary issues. Our shared convictions on those primary doctrines, contained in Scripture, are not negotiable. Oneness will not be found in organic union. The history of attempts of union between the denominations in the United Kingdom is a story of failure. Normally when two groups come together, the wings on either end of the union will then secede, creating three groups instead of two! Not once has union resulted in numerical growth, but always in decline.

We need to recognise that our distinctions are precious to us. Rather than merely conforming to each other we maintain different practices, but find that our essential unity is discovered in Christ Jesus. He alone provides the true ground of our oneness together.

I have often laughingly observed that if I was allowed to give a gold medal for services to evangelical unity I would have given it to David Jenkins, the former Bishop of Durham. I like and appreciate David, even though we confronted each other on the media over just about every issue imaginable concerning the person of Jesus Christ. The virgin birth, miracles, bodily resurrection, even the star in the east and the wise men proved to be the subject matter for our debates. Yet while this took place evangelical Christians grew closer to one another. For arguments over the raising of hands in worship, or the nature of the Holy Spirit's activity in our lives, paled into insignificance against the debate over whether the body of Jesus remained in a Middle Eastern tomb.

Our individual practices might divide us, but true unity was affirmed in defence of the nature of Jesus Christ. For he is the ground of truth and our unity together. It is Christ, as revealed in the Scriptures, who makes us one.

Jesus announced that he was the truth, his spirit would direct us into all truth, and this truth would set us free (John 8:32, 14:5, 16:13). He is the ground of our unity.

Some theologians today would seek to base an understanding of truth on the disposition of its advocate. They suggest that, in other words, 'I think it is true, because that is how I see it'. So no truth is regarded as absolute because it is given by God. All truth is relative and determined by my subjective opinion of what God would want from his people. One clear illustration of this comes in the way that scholars have suggested that Paul's insistence that Jesus is the 'one mediator between God and men' (1Timothy 2:5), and Peter's proclamation that 'salvation is found in no one else' (Acts 4:12) denote the language of testimony rather than theology. What is written speaks of their love rather than Christ's truth. Jesus was not 'absolutely the only', but 'the one whom we must take seriously' because of our commitment to him.[1]

In rejecting this opinion we unitedly affirm traditional understanding of Jesus. Evangelicals combine to affirm the Christ of biblical revelation. It is Jesus who alone brings forgiveness from sins and the offer of personal salvation (Mark 2:5–10; Luke 7:48; John 3:17; Acts 4:12, 5:31, 15:11; Galatians 1:4; Ephesians 5:25). He alone is the way to God, and now shares with his Father in the government of the universe (Acts 5:31, 10:42). This was the unanimous verdict of those who knew him and of the Holy Spirit who inspired the biblical writers. It was shared by the first Christians who clearly believed that Jesus was God, and they were prepared to die for their confidence in that fact. He was seen as unique, standing alone as the author of salvation and the fulfilment of prophecy (Acts 3:18, 25–6, 4:11, 10:43). They rejoiced in the conviction that he was now the ascended Lord (Acts 5:31).

The claim of Jesus was that he was the only way of salvation

(John 14:6). His followers clearly believed the same (Acts 16:31; Romans 10:9–13; Galatians 1:8; 1 Timothy 2:5). He also affirmed that other ways of salvation were false (John 8:19, 24, 41–7). His followers clearly concurred in this judgement (Acts 13:39, 17:21–33, 26:17–18; Romans 10:9–15; 1 Corinthians 10:20; 1 Thessalonians 1:9).

This affirmation remains distinctly uncongenial to our modern mood. Contemporary views were well represented when the TV presenter, Anne Diamond, applied the old adage, 'it doesn't matter what you believe, just so long as you are sincere about it!' She must have been supremely confident that only the most bigoted of viewers would object.

Yet this statement reduces the content of faith to irrelevance, and the authenticity of our religious feelings become all-important. Here evangelicals will unite in their profound disapproval. Such concepts may nowadays be 'politically correct' but they fall far short of the biblical insistence on truth.

(ii) One with other faiths?

Religious intolerance, wars, bigotry and hatred have all contributed to a common way of thinking that religion remains one area where we are not entitled to disagree with each other. This view is enhanced by the fact that today we live in a multi-faith society. My family has discovered that living in a South London street can produce its own complications. A Muslim up the road, a Hindu down the road, Buddhists and Sikhs around the corner, Catholics and Protestants in alternate houses – then the Jehovah's Witnesses knocking at the door, while the Mormons are visiting in the next street. When it comes to religion there is little shortage of choice! Presented with this kaleidoscope of belief, it is unsurprising that many confess to slight confusion.

It is easy to conclude that each must be addressing the same basic issues from a similar standpoint, but recruiting for their own cause. Confronted by such a huge variety of religious options it has become easy to suggest that everyone is entitled to their own choice. Therefore, surely, no single faith should be allowed to assume that it alone is right, and the others wrong! The verdict of our society has been that all faiths should learn to get along together. Therefore, in multi-faith societies like Britain, Australia and the USA among many others, what is needed is shared religious worship, especially on civic and state occasions. It is frequently argued that as every faith has emerged from its own culture and tradition, each must be as valid as the other. Instead of asserting superiority, different faiths could explore means of uniting with one another.

September 1993, and Chicago witnessed an extraordinary event. Just under 8,000 people gathered for a parliament of world religions. The Dalai Lama, Archbishops Desmond Tutu and Bernardin, the Roman Catholic theologian Hans Küng, and Swami Prakashanand Saraswati, joined with a host of religious luminaries to celebrate the first 1893 parliament of this kind, also held in Chicago.

The mood was buoyant and optimistic. Even impartial observers had predicted that it would

> undoubtedly be an influential and highly significant milestone in the continuing evolution of inter-religious relations ... Not only will it give concrete and attractive expression to what is emerging as a kind of consensus among many currently involved in inter-religious dialogue but it will certainly help to mould the nature of inter-religious relations as we head into the twenty-first century.[2]

A wide spectrum of religious belief was represented. This ranged from the mainline monotheistic faiths of Islam, Judaism and Christianity to the Eastern religions of Shintoism, Sikhism, Hinduism, Jainism, Taoism and Buddhism. Even cults like Scientology and neo-pagan faiths such as the ancient worship of Wicca were incorporated into the 'parliament'.

The Dalai Lama, as religious leader of the Tibetan people, urged the priority of spiritual development in a world where materialism has wreaked havoc with humanitarian values. His call for harmony and peace was reiterated by many others – but unity proved to be more fragile than anticipated.

Indian Hindus protested about the observations of Muslims and Sikh speakers attempted to 'rush the platform' to make their concerns known. The Greek Orthodox host committee from the Chicago Diocese withdrew from the parliament over the participation of the adherents of Wicca, an earth religion centred around the practice of witchcraft. They were particularly concerned with the involvement of the high priestess of the fellowship of Isis in the opening plenary blessings. Division also occurred between Islamic and Jewish attenders, causing more to withdraw. Such difficulties should not be surprising. For this ambitious project was based upon a simple reaffirmation of the statement from Swami Vivek-ananda to the 1893 parliament that, 'We believe not only in universal toleration, but we accept all religions to be true.'

More than a century later such sentiments evoke warm approval from the majority of contemporary society. They fit in well with the spirit of easy-going toleration which is prevalent in our modern world. It has become easy to assume that, at their heart, all religions must be basically the same!

This view insists that the truths of all religions are complemen-tary to one another. Therefore Buddhist priest and Christian clergy can freely worship together at a peace pagoda in the Midlands, for both roads ultimately lead to the same God or gods. To speak of unity should, from this perspective, address the unity of all faiths. Many contemporary Christian theologians have adopted a 'wheel' theory, suggesting that all religions provide complemen-tary paths to God. They are like the spokes of a wheel leading to its central hub. This inclusivist approach is adopted by the Roman Catholic Karl Rahner who speaks of 'anonymous Christians'. He argues that Christians are right to affirm Christ as the only way to God, but suggests that other faiths were in fact following him already, though unconsciously, and by employing different names. The implication is that 'we are all one in Christ Jesus', for every-one is a Christian whether they realise it or not. In similar vein Raymon Panniker assures us of a 'cosmic Christ' who informs all world religions. Another theologian, W. Cantwell Smith, has defended the idea of the mission of God's Spirit being fulfilled through Islam and Hinduism alongside Christianity.[3] Hans Küng has also suggested that we should search for echoes and reflections of the spirit of Jesus in others' faiths. He prescribed two forms of salvation. The ordinary way is open to the majority who have never been meaningfully exposed to Christianity and the extraordi-nary way is reserved for the comparative few who have encoun-tered Christ.

These views point to a basic unity of all religions, but their oneness is *in* Jesus Christ. What these ideas ignore is that other religions – even if they accept the idea of salvation – reject the notion that Jesus Christ is their means of receiving it! They see this offer of Christian citizenship as unasked for and unwanted.

This 'inclusive' position readily opens the door to the full-blooded pluralism of those who, like the philosopher John Hick, see God as the centre around which religious 'planets' revolve. Christianity is merely one of them. In a recent symposium twelve authors argued that all world religions exist on a par with one another. Each possesses equal validity in presenting different aspects of a universal human experience of spirituality.[4]

Here again we are presented with a model of unity, but this time apart from Jesus Christ. Its affirmation is that the 'truth element' of faith is irrelevant, it is our religious feelings that count – and these we share in common together. These ideas are both popular and attractive. Yet they reduce the concept of truth to the level of personal sincerity and conviction, and unity to a shared sense of religious consciousness. While this may well appeal to our sense of fair play it offers nothing to those engaged in a genuine search for truth and reality.

Representatives of Islam and Christianity alike object to the idea that the two should ever be regarded as equally correct. We agree that their conflicting claims require examination rather than indifference – for both cannot be right. Unity between those of different faiths is only possible at the level of shared humanity, for our beliefs are mutually contradictory.

(iii) United we stand

It is here that evangelical Christians will demonstrate their intrinsic unity. While we may be divided in our styles of worship, or forms of church government, a basic unity of conviction lies at the heart of our combining together.

Once it was our attitude to Scripture that seemed the primary distinctive of evangelicalism. That remains true, but in tomorrow's world it may prove to be our attitude to other faiths that will also demonstrate the clear separation between our views, and those of others within the Christian Church.

For the vast majority of evangelical opinion is united in five

clear-cut responses to the prevailing climate of contemporary
opinion.

(a) We agree that pluralism is bad news for the Church Democracy
insists that different beliefs and value systems should co-exist
together. On this judgement all will agree, each individual should
be free to choose their own standpoint as to the beliefs and values
they wish to live by. This mutual tolerance and freedom of choice
can be termed 'pluralism'.

However, the implications of pluralism proceed several steps too
far for evangelicals to concede. For it is assumed that all beliefs
and values are equal, and therefore no particular belief is right or
wrong. Truth, delusion and falsehood do not enter the equation,
all is reduced to the level of personal opinion.

Contrary to this world view lies the clear insistence of Christian
conviction:

- Jesus is completely unique, he alone is Son of God (John
  1:1-2, 20:28; Romans 9:5; Titus 2:13; Hebrews 1:8; 2 Peter
  1:1), and deserves our worship, prayer and trust (Matthew
  28:17; Acts 7:59, 9:13-19; Revelation 5:12).
- The Bible is divinely inspired and alone reveals the way that
  God intends us to live in his world (Psalm 19:7-14; Matthew
  4:4-10; Galatians 1:11-12; 2 Timothy 3:14-17).
- God's truth is absolute and unchangeable, his moral requirements apply to the whole of humankind, because each person
  is made in the image of God (Genesis 1:27; Colossians 3:10;
  James 3:9).

This stands in direct opposition to contemporary opinion which
views religious perspectives as beliefs rather than facts. For this
reason pluralism resulted in religious views being largely excluded
from public life. Politics and religion are kept strictly separate,
with no significant place being found for religious belief in parliament or the City, the town hall or the boardroom. It is rightly
observed that to the popular mind, 'Religious belief, far from
addressing the most important questions in life is a minority
"leisure" interest'.[5]

For the evangelical Christians such a view is unacceptable. Beliefs are not merely personal whims, nor are each equally correct. Whether the world's hungry are fed or our nation becomes great are not unimportant beliefs, and where they clash – both cannot be correct.

Truth does matter, and either we find it within ourselves or through God. Nor is knowledge of God's will reserved for Christians, therefore only needing to be practised by them. Even those who are unaware of the gospel still have the revelation of God contained in conscience, nature and creation (Psalm 19:1–6; Romans 1:19–20). Failure to see that God is the one to whom we must answer does not excuse anyone (Romans 2:14–15).

(b) We agree that Christianity is not to be reduced to the level of a privatised faith So evangelicals, united in their hostility towards pluralism are frustrated at being marginalised from ethical and social issues. Recognising that for many years in the twentieth century we were content to seek to retain our faith within a comfortable self-imposed 'ghetto-mentality' this trend is now being reversed. A burgeoning number of evangelical churches and para-church societies have become involved in providing care and support for the elderly, homeless, poor and disadvantaged. No longer can evangelicals be caricatured as a mere 'moral majority'. For concern on behalf of the unborn and the unemployed now march hand-in-hand. A growing involvement in parent teacher associations, community groups, and local and national government reflects a similar concern that evangelical faith can never be restricted to activities within an ecclesiastical building. The twentieth-century process of secularisation meant that church and society were separated from each other, yet today's evangelicals are seeking again to ensure that their voice is heard in the corridors of power. Concern for biblical moral values and standards of justice and intervention for the weak and oppressed highlight the growing conviction that together we have a role to play.

The activities of Tear Fund, Care, Shaftesbury Society, Causeway and many others all serve to illustrate the growing contribution that evangelicals can make towards the needs of society. Similarly, where majority evangelical views of biblical truth (as in areas like homosexual practice or abortion) are ignored their voice is increasingly raised to offer a different perspective. For Christian faith is viewed as being concerned with the whole of human life, not just the 'religious bits'.

(c) **We agree that all religions are not the same** While still at school my daughter Vicky was one of those responsible for running the Christian Union. The school also had a fairly large Islamic Society. The suggestion was made that a debate could take place between the two groups, and an external representative of Islam, and one for Christianity, could be found.

I therefore found myself pitted against a young Islamic scholar in the school hall one lunchtime. We did not spend time agreeing with each other. Neither of us found it necessary to do more than extend courtesy and respect to our opposing viewpoints. For as I was able to point out, 'Muslims believe that Jesus was a prophet, Christians maintain that he was, and is, the Son of God. Muslims point to a moral and religious code that is to be followed and obeyed, Christians look to a personal relationship with a God who comes to indwell their lives. Mohammed is still in the grave, and has been for over a thousand years, Christians believe that Jesus is alive, and can still be encountered today.'

No one was offended by this exchange of views. Nobody engaged in violent actions in support of contradictory viewpoints. There was simply a reasonable debate, for impartiality can be more offensive than convictions especially where a neutral view insists that conflicting perspectives are actually the same thing! For true tolerance of different ideas should never consist of blindness to the distinctive points they present. To pretend that all faiths are the same is to fail to do justice to their own perspectives. Such myopia is far more offensive than courteous disagreement.

Sometimes it is suggested that only extremists will choose to highlight the differences beween those of different faiths. It is true that followers of the Bahai faith would plead for mutual tolerance and forbearance between religions by accepting each other's position as a positive contribution to the whole. Hindus believe that all faiths essentially point in the same direction. However, many Muslims, Jews and Christians disagree with this analysis, believing in the exclusive claims of their own particular faith. It is hard to pretend that all are simply the same when, at its most basic level, Islam, Judaism and Christianity maintain that there is one

God, others believe in many! Hinduism points to a multiplicity of gods, while Buddhists search for ultimate reality within themselves, and Jains believe that God inhabits everything. One leading expert on mission has put it this way:

> Truth is not a matter of pride or humility. It is a matter of fact. Islam says Jesus wasn't crucified. We say he was. Only one of us can be right. Judaism says Jesus was not the Messiah. We say he was. Only one of us can be right. Hinduism says that God has *often* been incarnate. We say only once. And we can't both be right ... Any intelligent person could decide that all religions are wrong. Any intelligent person could decide that one is right and the rest wrong. But no intelligent person can seriously believe that all religions are essentially the same.[6]

Instead of presenting all faiths as equal or identical intellectual honesty demands that we recognise the disunity which prevails among religiously-minded people. How we handle our disagreements should be the true hallmark of tolerance, not how we avoid them, or pretend that they do not exist.

(d) We agree that tolerance and endorsement are not the same thing Whenever the Church has adopted restrictive practices it has only damaged itself. The nightmare of the Crusades and the Inquisition only illustrate the destructive consequences of adopting a policy of oppression. For the Kingdom of God can never be advanced by violent means.

We follow a Lord who advocated non-violent means of response in order that we might love our enemies, and employ different methods to propagate another kind of kingdom (Matthew 5:44, 26:52, John 18:36). Crucified truth oppresses no one, for we do not operate with this world's weapons (2 Corinthians 10:4).

Christianity therefore maintains the principle of legal tolerance, recognising the religious and political rights of every minority. It affirms the need for those who would disagree to have their freedom to protest, practise and propagate to be adequately protected in law. The intrinsic human rights should never be denied or abused. Furthermore, Christians will maintain the need for social tolerance. The self-determination of every individual must be respected, because God respects it. He does not impose his will on anyone, and nor must we. To call down fires of judgement on those with whom we disagree is never to be permitted (Luke 9:54–5). Recognising that all human beings are God's creation, and bear his image, we are to respect all persons, whatever their views may be, seeking to understand and appreciate their position.

Such legal and social tolerance should never be allowed to deprive us of the right to disagree, and to seek to convince another of the error of their stated position. To pretend that all views will ultimately concur is to practise an intellectual tolerance which, in its extreme position, is foolishness. This kind of all-embracing tolerance will be held by those whose pluralist view is 'concerned with the way other religions might be brought into some kind of larger ecumenical relationship where the truths of each are seen as complementary to each other'.[7]

With this perspective evangelicals will profoundly disagree. As John Stott has acutely observed, 'To cultivate a mind so broad that it can tolerate every opinion, without ever detecting anything in it to reject, is not a virtue; it is the vice of the feeble-minded. It can degenerate into an unprincipled confusion of truth with error and goodness with evil.'[8]

The heartbeat of tolerance is not a bland indifference to distinctive positions, or a woolly-minded compromise which fudges the real issues. True tolerance lies in knowing how to agree to disagree, holding our understanding of truth with love – while demonstrating grace in the middle of comprehensive disagreement.

Religious belief must never be regarded as being above criticism. When the Indian 'Thugs' demonstrated their passionate devotion to the goddess Kali by murdering innocent victims their actions could never be condoned as 'part of their religion'! Justice had to be employed against their murderous practices. When Islam persecutes Christian believers we are not entitled to view such happenings with indifference. We have to use the arguments of justice and freedom of conscience on behalf of those who are oppressed.

Nor can we blindly ignore the conflict of ideology between Christians and those of other faiths. Instead of being content to separate ourselves from the situation we have the obligation to present the truth of the Christian faith. Indifference is not an option to which we are entitled.

Authentic Christianity will always welcome a dialogue with those who disagree with it. We can agree with the right of non-Christians to practise their faith, but we must always demand the equal freedom to voice our disagreement. For we can be tolerant without compromise, permit freedom of action without being mealy-mouthed about our faith.

(e) **We agree that conversion lies at the heart of the Christian faith** A Greek Catholic Bishop in Galilee wrote in his farewell letter that, 'As a Bishop, a preacher of the Gospel, I never tried to convert a Jew or Arab Moslem to Christianity; rather to convert them to be a better Jew, a better Moslem'.[9] This represents a fantastic misreading of the New Testament, for if the early preachers of the gospel had adopted that policy the Christian Church would not exist today.

The Early Church grew through conversion of Jews and pagans alike. The Christian commitment to conversion went back to the Damascus road, and the dramatic transformation in the life of Saul of Tarsus. This was a story he related to Jews and Romans alike, insisting on the need he had of a personal encounter with God (Acts 22:1–21, 26:4–18). While he retained the culture and training of Judaism he unflinchingly preached the need for Jewish people to meet Jesus. In Athens Paul confronted ideas of a multiplicity of gods and insisted that there was one God who can be encountered in Jesus Christ (Acts 17:22–31), because he has risen from the dead. He was absolutely convinced of the truth of this message, dismissing all rival opinion as lies (Galatians 1:9). The uniqueness of Jesus and his offer of salvation was the content of the message conveyed by the early Christians. As Michael Green has observed,

> The early preachers did not enter into dialogue with the world, except to understand it and to present their life-changing message in terms comprehensible to their contemporaries. They believed they had got good news for their friends, and they knew that good news was embodied in Jesus Christ. Him they proclaimed.[10]

In stark contrast stands a recent report which comments that after the Decade of Evangelism was launched, 'Other British faith communities expressed fears that their members might be singled out as targets for conversion ... In response, reassurances were given by church leaders that the primary goals of the Decade are the rekindling of the faith of nominal Christians and the drawing in of those with no existing religious commitment.'[11] It is difficult to reconcile this statement with that of Paul when he declared, 'Woe to me if I do not preach the gospel' (1Corinthians 9:16). If our missionary predecessors of the nineteenth century had regarded the conversion of those of other faiths inappropriate then half of the current Christian church worldwide would still be unconverted.

Christians will recognise that those of other faiths will disagree with us, but that should never prohibit sensitive but uncompromising efforts to lead them to Jesus.

It is here that the roots of evangelical unity lie deepest. We are committed to the truth of the gospel and of the principle that freedom of religion should include the right to seek to propagate it. For the Christian faith is a missionary faith that spreads by personal conversion, not by military takeover or collective indoctrination.

We are therfore tired of the abuse and vilification offered by a pluralist society. We agree that the Christian message must be shared in a loving and demonstrable way, but the gospel cannot be gagged. We know that past generations have died for this freedom and we are prepared to pay whatever price is necessary to see it retained.

This then is our unity – it is not just contained in our fellowship together, or our common beliefs and practices, but in a mutual commitment to maintain the exclusive claims of Christ against the rising tide of pluralism. For despite our willingness to be inclusive in sharing with the needs of the suffering and dispossessed, and in offering Christian truth to all who would embrace it, we will acknowledge our exclusivism in four cardinal areas. Evangelicals are united because:

- We insist on the supreme authority of Scripture.
- We insist on the unique redemption available through Christ's death.

– We insist on the need for personal conversion.
– We insist on the urgent necessity for evangelism.[12]

While these unite us as evangelicals, they will by their nature divide us from others. Our response is not to compromise our distinctives, but to seek to persuade others that these alone offer the way to become 'all one in Christ Jesus'.

5

Fracture points

The fact that evangelicals have a high regard for truth brings with it a recurring danger. Our firmly held convictions can cause us to become highly fractious and prone to division. Of all the armies of the Christian church, the evangelicals have most often made a habit, or in some cases almost a virtue, of fighting one another. It has become a time-honoured evangelical custom to shoot ourselves in the foot. By the time an evangelical spokesperson has escaped the minefields set by fellow evangelicals, it can seem extraordinary that he or she is not too weary or wounded to have any appetite for wider debate in defence of the faith.

Predestination and free will

We can readily identify a number of reefs on which evangelical unity in previous generations has been regularly prone to shipwreck, both sides appealing confidently to the Bible in defence of their position. Among the most notable is the Calvinist/Arminian conflict. The underlying controversy has recurred across the centuries, notably in Augustine's dispute with Pelagius and then Luther's with Erasmus. This dispute about God's sovereignty and human free will was sharpened by the rigorous systematics of Calvin, and further intensified by subsequent Calvinists and the leading exponent of the alternative perspective, Arminius. Above all, this was the great evangelical debate that rocked the eighteenth-century Awakening in Britain and America.

At a time of unprecedented advance and responsiveness to the gospel, opinions hardened on both sides as this controversy moved to centre stage. The great champions of mass evangelism, Wesley and Whitefield, expended valuable time and energy on combative preaching and writing against one another. Their followers often took the initiative in the hostilities, their devotion to the support of the preacher who had brought them much personal blessing led to unwarranted polemical attacks against fellow believers. What began in preaching the spilt blood of Christ risked declining into the spillage of one another's blood, not with physical but with verbal violence, which could only dishonour the Lord they all claimed to love and serve. Issues that needed thorough exploration in informed theological debate were often tackled publicly through denunciation and caricature, with no room for subtlety or nuances of interpretation. Both positions plainly led, and can still lead, to excess: a hyper-Arminianism that knows no assurance of salvation and is driven by an excessive and overwhelming sense of personal obligation to win the world, and a hyper-Calvinism that proves arrogant and pharisaical about election and can be indifferent to the need to take action in response to the Great Commission.

In recent decades, views have become more fluid, though the interpretations of this trend have stirred their own controversy. While some berate a growing doctrinal anaemia and biblical illiteracy, others are delighted by a new preparedness to break free from old entrenchments. A new softening away from old polarisations is reflected in the emergence of many who are broadly reformed in theology, but decline to accept the stricter tenets of Calvinist doctrine, notably the limited atonement and predestination to perdition. Similarly, a number who are broadly Arminian have come to grant some kind of place to the sovereignty of God. Nonetheless, even though relatively dormant at present, this divergence remains ever present, an irreducible crux of dispute. The paradoxical tensions of the biblical data cannot be avoided or readily resolved, and so beneath the surface the debate still simmers.

The fact that this controversy is there to stay can be illustrated from among the new churches. Ichthus and Pioneer are devoted champions of Arminianism, and some of their more prominent leaders seem quite prepared to throw down a polemical gauntlet before even moderately reformed evangelicals. Indeed, some show a marked reluctance in any circumstances to speak affirmatively of the sovereignty of God, possibly in reaction against an arid hyper-Calvinism encountered in their pre-charismatic days. However, this should not be taken to imply that the charismatic movement or the new churches are universally Arminian. The same divergence is found here as in the rest of the evangelical world. New Frontiers, for example, are pleased not only to make explicit reference to both predestination and the sovereign work of God in their Bible teaching, but also to celebrate the doctrine of predestination in their worship songs.

Part of our problem over many generations in the West is almost certainly a cultural reluctance, or even inability, to align ourselves with Hebrew patterns of thought. Jesus and Paul confidently assert both human free will and divine sovereignty, without any apparent need to reconcile these two propositions. In Greek thought, however, such apparently contrary assertions need to be systematised into a single and integrated perspective. The almost inevitable result of applying a Greek mind set to Hebrew thought is that one of these apparently conflicting propositions is sacrificed in the defence of the other, or alternatively, they are blended together into some kind of diluted compromise, with the result that justice is done to neither.

The end of the world

During the nineteenth and early twentieth centuries, millenarian controversies moved to centre stage. It became a matter of fundamental concern and division among Christians whether the second coming would occur before or after the millennium, the thousand years of the triumphant reign of God's kingdom on earth. In the case of some pre-millennial schools, further controversies centred around the exact nature and timetabling of the events leading up to Christ's return to inaugurate the millennium. These controversies that were once matters of critical and heated debate have largely fallen from view, but not because the doctrinal and exegetical issues have always been resolved to the satisfaction of the disputants. Some even object that the growth of indifference with regard to the future indicates a sell-out to the spirit of the age: an often accidental or unconscious conformity with the existentialist priority of 'living in the now'.

Scholarly questions have been raised about the weight of significance that has been attached to the reference to a thousand years in Revelation 20. If the thousand years is rightly understood as a symbolic figure, rather than a literal statement referring to 365,000 days, then the entire interpretative schema of both pre- and post-millennialism is shaken. As a result, many evangelical scholars have led the way in developing an agnostic amillennialism. We know that Christ is coming again, as judge of every woman and man, but as to the specifics, many are now more willing to conclude that these are beyond our present capacity to know or interpret with the precision once presumed.

In popular evangelicalism, there has been a steady increase in indifference to these old concerns, rejecting the rigid certitudes of eschatological timetabling championed by previous generations of evangelicals. To some, these former controversies are treated with contempt, seen as the barren product of an evangelical scholasticism, a wasteland as arid as the learned medieval speculations about the number of angels able to dance upon a single pinhead. In short, a fruitless exercise in abstruse learning, without wisdom or profit.

Others are concerned about the critical connection between beliefs and behaviour. They remind us that a primary purpose of biblical prophecy is to have an ethical impact in the present. The prophets do not predict the future merely to give us an inside track on the destiny of the human race. Rather, the predictive element of prophecy is always accompanied by immediate demands upon our lifestyle. The central intent of biblical teaching on the second coming is not to provoke rigorous examination of various schedules for the events of the last days. Instead, faced with clear teaching upon the return of Christ as King, we are invited to ask the question, 'In the light of the revealed and certain end of history, by what priorities should we be living now?'

Varieties of church

Though the great reformers produced a revolution in the church, calling Christians back to grace alone and the Scriptures alone, they patently failed to produce a single, evangelical model of church life. As a result evangelicals have naturally disagreed ever since on issues of denominational churchmanship. Without dwelling on the individual debates, we can identify the following familiar and recurrent disputes:

the legitimacy of a state church,
the nature of Christian ministry – priests or not?
baptism – of infants or believers?
a set liturgy – invaluable resource or terrible snare?
local church government – by clergy, elders or people?
the legitimacy and authority of the episcopacy,
independence, relational connections or a wider Church beyond the local?

None of these debates has been resolved. As a result of the passing of the years without the slightest indication of an emerging consensus, we have learned to agree to differ. Rather than not talking any more, we have tacitly conceded not to return too often to old contentions.

To the pervasive framework of divergence outlined above, the rise of liberalism within in the late nineteenth century provoked new calls for evangelicals to separate from inclusive denominations. Spurgeon's call for separation from the Baptist Union is an obvious historical precedent for Lloyd-Jones' more wide-ranging exhortations in the mid-twentieth century.

It now becomes a serious question how far those who abide by the faith once delivered to the saints should fraternize with those who have turned aside to another gospel ... It is one thing to overleap all boundaries of denominational restriction for the truth's sake; this we hope all godly men will do more and more. It is quite another policy which would urge us to subordinate the maintenance of truth to denominational prosperity and unity. Numbers of easy-minded people wink at error so long as it is committed by a clever man and a good-natured brother, who has so many fine points about him.[1]

One thing is clear to us: we cannot be expected to meet in any union which comprehends those whose teaching upon fundamental points is exactly the reverse of that which we hold dear ... With deep regret we abstain from assembling with those whom we dearly love and heartily respect, since it would involve us in a confederacy with those with whom we can have no fellowship in the Lord.[2]

The notorious public disagreement of Martyn Lloyd-Jones and John Stott at the Evangelical Alliance Assembly in 1966, is a pertinent illustration of unresolved differences of churchmanship among evangelicals. As the evangelical movement began to move beyond the experience of being a beleaguered remnant in the post-war years, liberal theology became steadily more radical and outspoken, with the rise of the Death of God theology, or more accurately anti-theology. In this ferment, where evangelicals were beginning to engage once again in serious theological debate within the academic world, Stott and Lloyd-Jones drew opposite conclusions. For Lloyd-Jones, contending for the faith pointed towards a clear and uncompromised evangelical separatism. For Stott, the resurgence of evangelicalism was a basis not for departure from, but to work for reform within the historic and mixed denominations. Faced with Lloyd-Jones' impassioned eloquence, Stott felt obliged to repudiate the fiery rhetoric with the observation that church history stood squarely against the effectiveness of separatism.

A more detached historian might have observed that there is equally little or no historical precedent for the attempted evangelical reform of existing denominations which has characterised the last thirty years since that confrontation. In the heat of the moment, both were skating on thin ice. With the benefit of hindsight it would have been much better to have tackled such issues not through a sermon but through a properly planned and structured debate, with papers from leading exponents of both positions and a frank recognition that neither position could in all honesty lay claim to being the sole legitimate repository of the evangelical consensus. It is to be hoped that time has healed the wounds and a re-examination of the issues today would not require the same outcome, in which much evangelical opinion polarised into two camps, the separatists viewing the reformers as naïve and compromised, the reformers viewing the separatists as naïve and divisive.

Present threats to evangelical unity

Today evangelicals are resurgent in the British churches. Although this results from our own numerical growth, it also derives from the continuing and catastrophic decline across much of the rest of church life. Numerical strength may prove increasingly hazardous for evangelicals. When we are few, we tend to stick together. The more numerous we become, the greater the temptation to divide from one another. We can identify a range of debates that have come to the fore in recent years as potential rocks of division.

1) Charismatic renewal

In the early days of Pentecostalism, the vituperative denunciations by evangelicals were horrendous. In Britain, one leading and highly respected Bible teacher cursed Pentecostals as 'the last vomit of Satan'. In Germany evangelicals formulated the Berlin Declaration, which explicitly and categorically decreed that such experiences and the so-called spiritual gifts had nothing to do with the Holy Spirit. It is a matter of the deepest regret in international evangelicalism that such an unwarranted and intemperate official statement is still waiting to be unreservedly repudiated with fulsome apologies and repentance.

When it comes to evaluating the spiritual gifts, particularly tongues, prophecy and healing, Pentecostalism at the beginning of the century and charismatic renewal in the sixties broke upon an evangelical world much influenced by pre-millennial dispensationalism. According to this school, in the present dispensation, beyond the apostolic age, authentic spiritual gifts have altogether ceased. From this pre-conceived position, with the assumption that it faithfully represented biblical teaching, it was inevitable that a dogmatic assertion would follow: such activities may derive from the flesh, or may come from Satan, but the source could not possibly be the Spirit of God!

Dispensationalism is now on the wane, recognised as a relatively recent fundamentalist construct rather than an accurate interpretation of the biblical data. Cessationism likewise appears to be in rapid decline, not only because it becomes immediately less plausible severed from the construct of dispensationalism, but also because it has lost credibility. The witness of history refutes the assertion that any of the spiritual gifts at all were in truth restricted to the era of the first apostles. At the same time, the extensive eruptions of spiritual gifts across the denominations and around the world have been accompanied by the clear preaching of the gospel and the fruit of both conversions and holy living. Indeed the Pentecostals are the most rapidly growing churches worldwide. Faced with such a wealth of evidence of authentic Christian vitality, the old cessationist claims have moved from being initially persuasive for many evangelicals, through a period of increasing implausibility, until in the nineties they have become no less than ludicrous, demonstrably falsified in countless churches and countries.

The continued numerical growth of charismatics is changing the balance of evangelicalism. Just as statistical projections for the future of the Protestant churches looks increasingly evangelical, the future of evangelicalism looks increasingly charismatic. Old hostilities may have waned, but the growing numbers of charismatics will lead inevitably to a continuing shift in the evangelical consensus. This may provoke some entrenched anti-charismatics to become more outspoken in their attacks, more sweeping in their denunciations, seeking in a rearguard action to drive a wedge between evangelical and charismatic convictions, arguing that the two positions are mutually exclusive and irreducibly opposed to one another.

Since renewal is intrinsically ground breaking and experimental, charismatic evangelicals will often explore unfamiliar territory. They are the pioneers of evangelicalism. This means that a fair number of mistakes are quite inevitable, and these need to be freely acknowledged. Some charismatics may seem addicted to novelty, fashion prone and even gullible in their rapid and enthusiastic adoption of the latest spiritual guru. Others show illuminist tendencies, leaning towards a kind of neo-gnosticism, an existentialist hyper-subjectivism, in which everything is reduced to intuitive hunches, with no place for reasoned examination or biblical evaluation. Issues related to the principles and practice of healing, deliverance and spiritual warfare could all prove flash points for controversy and dispute. In each case, when practitioners see exciting results, it is tempting to produce an over-speculative theory, attempting to give a comprehensive account of the hidden mechanics of supernatural events. The result is that gullible enthusiasts accept all too readily the latest fashionable theory, which often bears little relation to the biblical verses from which it is notionally derived.

We also detect a measure of charismatic identity crisis. For some, charismatic is treated as a noun, distinct from evangelical: 'I am a charismatic and an evangelical.' The two identities are considered quite separate, complementary but distinct. For a second group, their entry into renewal has entailed a sometimes painful departure from a hardline anti-charismatic church. For such Christians, their own experience may lead them to assert, 'I was once an evangelical, but now I am a charismatic.' For a third group, 'charismatic' is considered an adjective, providing a distinctive nuance to a continuing evangelical identity: 'I am a charismatic evangelical, that is, an evangelical with a charismatic flavour.' On the whole, the third perspective has increasingly become the consensus position. The exponents of this third position will do the greatest service to their fellow evangelicals (charismatic, non-charismatic and anti-charismatic) if in the next few years they can demonstrate that they are genuinely maturing into a movement which, in recovering the presence, gifts and power of the Holy Spirit, remains fully and unreservedly evangelical in roots, convictions and priorities.

In short, charismatics will inevitably stir controversy, but it is to be hoped that they will become increasingly self-critical as the movement matures. The rest of the evangelical world has often looked to the charismatics for surprises. Perhaps the time is coming when they will also be looked to for both self-criticism and visionary leadership, genuinely and creatively integrating the twin priorities of the Word and the Spirit.

2) Infallible or inerrant

Concerned that the customary evangelical word to describe the authority of Scripture, that is 'infallibility', was becoming debased by too many qualifications, some evangelical leaders, mainly in the United States, sought to introduce more precision with the term 'inerrancy'. In truth this debate has never really taken hold this side of the Atlantic, where many feared that the controversy would provoke needless division over an issue of little more than mere semantics. Nonetheless, the authority of Scripture, no matter how inspiration is defined, is always under attack. Defending this unique, revelatory authority and clarifying the nature of biblical inspiration remains a continuing evangelical priority.

This debate reveals further facets of evangelical diversity. On the right wing are the fundamentalists, but we need to recognise that while all fundamentalists are evangelical, not all evangelicals are fundamentalist. The non-fundamentalist evangelical will argue for a more subtle and nuanced understanding of biblical inspiration, interpreting the books of the Bible according to their various genres and the intentions of the original authors. On the left wing, some who wish to continue to be identified as evangelicals have blurred beyond all recognition the evangelical understanding of biblical inspiration, authority and reliability. Though the term 'inerrancy' has not succeeded in resolving the issue, its attempted introduction highlights a searching question: when does an evangelical's approach to the Bible mean that they have ceased to be recognisable as an authentic evangelical?

3) Hermeneutics

We cannot turn from the fracture points concerned with the authority of the Bible without recognising the contribution and controversy surrounding the principles of biblical interpretation or hermeneutics. On the one hand, hermeneutics seeks to avoid and indeed repudiate the arbitrary subjectivism of those who wrench Bible verses not only from their context within a biblical book, but also from the original setting. This larger context includes more than the culture of the time and the genre of the book, though these dimensions both profoundly shape the significance of any document. Modern analysis also recognises that we must take account of what the original author sought to communicate and what the original recipients would have understood the text to mean. The intended and received meanings could, of course, potentially be quite distinct and even remote from each other.

Reliable biblical exposition must always take account of these principles, but we can identify several areas of potential conflict. Those convinced by the validity of these principles of interpretation will find unacceptable certain kinds of fundamentalist preaching, that claim to preach 'only the Bible', but in practice tend to read into the text concepts that are entirely alien in the context of the original setting. Only recently I encountered a well regarded preacher explaining with the help of numerous and elaborate diagrams how principalities and powers hold cities in their grip. Although his message made frequent reference to various verses from Ephesians, I was entirely unable to see that his elaborate cosmology bore any objective or direct connection with Pauline teaching. His use of the New Testament was well intentioned but entirely unconvincing, proof-texting his own ideas rather than a genuine exposition of biblical teaching. Proper principles of biblical interpretation require us to point out, at risk of contradiction and dispute, that such preaching, no matter how highly regarded among the people, is in fact not evangelical enough!

Problems arise not only among those who neglect these principles, for we can also identify major difficulties with their implementation. Firstly, the more complicated biblical interpretation becomes, the nearer we come to undoing a great principle of the Reformation. If modern evangelical scholarship produces techniques that require years of academic learning to master, we may repeat the error of the medieval church and take the Bible away from the people, with the implication that the untutored are not in a position to comprehend God's Word. While there is no excuse for anti-intellectualism, there is also no excuse for such quasi-priestly elitism, which represents a fundamental betrayal of evangelical convictions.

Secondly, in seeking to determine the most precise tools for biblical interpretation, we must not lose sight of the fact that while the Bible is a collection of ancient books, it also continues to impart divine revelation today. The texts do indeed have a specific cultural and historical setting and a specific message, but they are also the living Word of God, through which God speaks in a contemporary way to his people in every generation. He speaks not only through the careful studies of the theologically trained, but also directly, without the mediation of any other book or person.

Thirdly, despite the desire to exclude arbitrary and subjective distortions of the biblical text, there still results a considerable degree of diversity in biblical interpretation. Under the influence of structuralism and post-modernism, which have tended to devalue the very concept of objective meaning in any text, we can be faced with a new subjectivism, impressively learned and complex, but still shaped by the presuppositions and preferences of a particular interpreter.

Fourthly, when exploring the major ethical and theological controversies of the day, hermeneutic principles can be applied in such a way as to relativise the plain teaching of the Bible. That is, while a text may appear to make a direct, clear and absolute moral statement, we can reconstruct the original setting and appear to explain the absolute away. Our ingenuities of contextualisation conveniently turn the Ten Commandments which stand for ever, into ten tentative suggestions for a possible approach to life in a particular cultural and historical setting.

Official church reports that are presented as offering a thoughtful Christian and biblical perspective, increasingly display values that ape and echo our secular society. They may claim to be using objective principles of interpretation to handle the Bible correctly, but when they have finished the sacred text will have turned into the dust of religious relativism. If anyone attempts to contradict such views, they risk being swept aside as theologically unsophisticated or hermeneutically illiterate. The danger of such subjective excesses is that hermeneutics could leave us with an emasculated Bible, with no more objective meaning than the vocabulary of Lewis Carroll's master of re-interpretation, Humpty Dumpty:

'When *I* use a word,' Humpty Dumpty said in rather a scornful tone, 'it means just what I choose it to mean – neither more nor less.'

'The question is,' said Alice, 'whether you *can* make words mean so many different things.'

'The question is,' said Humpty Dumpty, 'which is to be master – that's all.'[3]

4) Established church
Throughout the West old institutions are being questioned. Time-honoured bastions of the establishment can no longer take for

granted their continued grip on power, or even their future existence. In Britain, the pressure continues to mount for a greater degree of independent government in Scotland and Wales. The House of Lords may not survive much longer as an unelected second chamber. In a modern egalitarian democracy, it appears increasingly not so much quaint, charming and archetypally British, but outmoded, elitist and unjustifiable. As the new century draws near, a growing number are reluctant to condone the retention of parliamentary power in the hands of a somnolent assemblage of hereditary peers together with the superannuated recipients of political preferment.

The royal family is also losing its grip on the popular imagination. The Windsors still fill the headlines, but in recent years this has been the result of scandal, rather than sentimental anecdotes and affectionate tributes. Even the Boy Scouts, often thought of as a thoroughly reactionary throwback to the days of imperial power, have begun to question gravely whether future scouts can reasonably be expected to promise 'to do my duty to God and the King', when, as a self-confessed adulterer, Prince Charles is hardly an ideal embodiment of loyalty and trustworthiness. Sadly, but perhaps not surprisingly, when the stories of Prince Charles' adultery first broke in the press, several Anglican bishops bent over backwards in their public statements, not in defence of the moral standards of the Ten Commandments, but rather in defence of the future head of their church, praising his honesty and sympathising with the exceptional pressures monarchy and the press had placed upon his marriage.

In this egalitarian and pragmatic age, the established church is not exempt from the climate of searching questions. Leading newspapers and senior politicians have begun to ask whether an established church has any continuing validity at all, in a multi-faith and secular society, especially when the Anglican church represents less than one third of churchgoers and the sum of churchgoers is less than 10 per cent of the adult population.

The political obstacles in the way of disestablishment are immense. Without a written constitution, the established church is woven into the fabric of national life. It is highly unlikely that any government would be prepared to give the enormous amount of legislative time required to bring about a systematic and complete severance. Nonetheless, establishment does seem increasingly inappropriate for a twenty-first century democracy. Therefore, if ever Britain does adopt a written constitution, whether as a nation state or as part of the European Community, it seems likely that the established church would be deemed expendable, even obsolete.

Although this debate has resurfaced in the nation, evangelicals have shown little interest thus far. Free churches seem to have lost their historic strength of conviction in favour of disestablishment. Rather than being opposed to establishment as a matter of principle, many have become pragmatic supporters of the status quo, arguing that Christian influence in a godless age is protected by the Church of England retaining its privileged position. Ironically, in recent years it has often been from within the state church, and frequently by evangelical Anglicans, that the case for disestablishment has most forcibly been made.

We have identified two trends in society: increasingly secular and increasingly egalitarian, with a widespread preparedness to question and even propose the abolition of long-hallowed institutions that are perceived to be no longer relevant. If this analysis is correct, the established church faces a rocky ride in the next quarter century. If debate begins to rage, especially after Prince Charles ascends the throne, it is inevitable that evangelicals will take both sides, and a long-standing contentious issue will become the storm centre for new controversy, both in the evangelical world and in the nation.

5) Ecumenism

Evangelical responses to structural ecumenism fall into three groups. The most voluble and most often noticed are the polar opposites: those who are enthusiastic participants and those who categorically repudiate the entire ecumenical process. Both groups have difficulty with the fact that fellow evangelicals have drawn the diametrically opposed conclusion. Roman Catholic participation in the new ecumenical instruments has raised the stakes, increasing the fervour and suspicion of the non-participants. While some evangelicals are pursuing new dialogue with Roman Catholics, others consider any degree of rapprochement to be nothing less than a betrayal of the Reformation.

The vast majority of evangelicals are found somewhere between these two extremes. They are neither convinced by the claim that biblical principles demand unqualified participation in ecumenical structures, nor by the claim that biblical integrity forbids entirely all manner of co-operation and dialogue. They remain unconvinced that the ecumenical instruments are the most significant Christian initiative in this generation, but nor do they believe them to be intrinsically disastrous. They therefore prefer to stay involved to a limited degree, seeking to speak out as evangelicals graciously and clearly, working to bring an evangelical influence within the ecumenical structures, just as non-separatist evangelicals have worked for biblical reform by staying involved in theologically diverse denominations. Their participation is cautious and pragmatic.

The moderate majority of evangelicals face double disapproval. From one wing they are considered half-hearted, failing to grant ecumenical events sufficient time and energy; from the other, any involvement at all represents a severe lapse in wise and principled behaviour. Whatever the measure of success enjoyed by official ecumenical initiatives in the coming years, they are here to stay, and so are the three schools of evangelical thought, keen ecumenical activists, zealous anti-ecumenists, and the non-combative moderate majority. It would be a great and tragic irony if recent initiatives to promote Christian unity had the accidental and indirect impact of provoking substantial evangelical division.

6) Social and political action

It is no longer contentious for evangelicals to insist on the vital importance of social action, but the Achilles' heel of the recovery of an evangelical social conscience has been a loss of urgency in evangelism. Witness the fact that the enormous increase in financial support by evangelicals for TEAR Fund over recent decades has been accompanied by a severe decline in support for missionary societies whose primary purpose is evangelistic. Our theology has insisted that social action and evangelism are both essential expressions of the gospel. Our giving continues to reveal an underlying tendency to pick and choose.

While the backwoodsmen still exist who will always remain dismissive of all social action, other evangelicals have been heard in recent years to suggest not merely that social action and evangelism are both needed, but more controversially that social action and evangelism are really one and the same. That is, if we provide care for our neighbour, this is an authentic and sufficient witness to the gospel. The logical outcome of this line of argument is that, so long as we are caring people, there is no need to speak about Christ and his cross at all, let alone explain the need for personal repentance and faith. Since Jesus not only demonstrated the love of God in action, above all in his healing ministry and personal counsel, but also preached good news both to the crowds and to individuals, we need to refute strenuously all misguided attempts to conflate social action and evangelism. Evangelism without social action lacks demonstration and credibility. Social action without explicit evangelism lacks explanation and ultimately even lacks the very love it seeks to express. The starving cannot eat Bibles, but nor can they receive eternal salvation without feeding on the bread of life.

As concern for social action probes the economic structures that lead to poverty, a shift occurs beyond compassion into searching questions about exploitation. For some, this is social action taken to its logical conclusion in a radical cry for justice, a necessary and prophetic unmasking of the roots of poverty. For others, this is thought to be nothing less than Marxism with a religious face, a completely unacceptable distortion of the biblical gospel. At one extreme we encounter a politicised kingdom theology in which the entire gospel is reconstructed in socio-political terms, a *Guardian*-reading, social democratic Christianity. Among full-time Christian leaders this is probably more prevalent than elsewhere in the Church. It is frequently a slightly nostalgic pre-Thatcherite moderate socialism, in which Mrs Thatcher becomes the unacceptable face of capitalism. Its exponents take it for granted that a right-of-centre perspective is innately unacceptable and ill-conceived. Left-of-centre convictions are assumed to be not only more just and compassionate, but also more biblical and more thinking.

Among the majority of Christians, however, recent surveys suggest that the most popular newspapers remain the *Telegraph* and the *Mail*. This leads many into an evangelical Toryism, in which such quasi-socialist Christian thinking is deeply unpalatable. For both groups of evangelical Christians, their own political persuasion is more or less taken for granted as natural and inevitable, the self-evident consequence of a biblical perspective. When both groups are self-assured about the obvious rightness of their own position, there is little room for manoeuvre. If British politics goes through a period of polarisation, perhaps with a particularly unpleasant period of blood-letting, evangelicals may find it difficult not to experience a similar polarisation in the socio-political arena.

7) Denominational identity
Evangelicals have been unable to agree concerning the relative status of their denominational setting and their evangelical convictions. A detailed examination of this issue is found in chapter 7. We also need to recognise the distinct possibility that some of the historic denominations may be close to abandoning key principles of Christian ethics in the next few years. Should this come about, for example with an abandonment of traditional Christian teaching against living together and homosexual practice, evangelicals will be obliged to ask whether the moment has come when principled separation is unavoidable.

Almost certainly, should such a crisis arise, there will not only be a division between evangelicals and their co-denominationalists, but also a division among evangelicals. Some will decide to stay within their denomination, loyal come what may, even at the risk of seriously compromising their evangelical convictions. Others will conclude that they have no choice but to leave, with considerable sadness and regret. A few may resolve to depart with a display of belligerence, denouncing their old denomination and declaring that the attempt to bring evangelical reform to the historic denominations was always more likely to encounter shipwreck than success.

8) The value and significance of new churches
Some evangelicals in the historic denominations have never come to terms with the existence of the new churches. Others more readily accept the fact that these churches represent an experimental cutting edge of mission in the modern world. In the coming decade we can expect a number of trends among the new churches, although we note in passing that having moved from being called house churches to new churches, as second generation leaders come

to prominence yet another new title will soon be required: when do new churches cease to be 'new'? Some are so anti-institutional that they will probably not survive long once their founders pass on the reins. Some will spawn a further generation of new churches, as younger leaders face the need for further radical re-inventions of the church in a rapidly changing culture. Others, despite long standing protestations that they are non-denominational will almost certainly establish structures that will turn them unmistakably from networks of local churches into new denominations. As the organisations become larger and more structured, it is likely to prove increasingly difficult to retain the distinctive quality of supportive relationships among leaders that has often characterised the new churches thus far.

If this prognosis is at all accurate, the following fracture points will increasingly emerge. Those who have never liked the new churches, or have been threatened by them, will be tempted to argue that the entire development was erroneous if, with the passing of years, new churches become additional denominations. Like Mark Twain reading his own obituary in the newspaper, the new churches will also have to put up with their death being announced prematurely. Some leaders in the historic denominations will inevitably assert that the new churches' time has passed and that future growth will be found mainly in the old channels. Present evidence suggests that, while growth is by no means restricted to their particular styles of fellowship and worship, the new churches are here to stay.

Within the new churches, some early enthusiasts declared that these new kinds of church were the only legitimate type and that their rediscovery would almost instantaneously usher in revival. It has been said that a cynic is a disappointed idealist, and there was certainly a great deal of naïve idealism, and even hype in the early years of the new churches. Some have already shown signs of becoming disillusioned or even cynical due to unfulfilled and naïve expectations. Others become confused when they see new church leaders working to develop constructive relationships with leaders in the historic denominations. Such co-operative initiatives are surely to be welcomed, but are no doubt confusing for those who previously left an historic denomination believing that nothing good was to be found there in future.

A further fracture point for evangelicals will arise from the gradual emergence of some new church streams into a more fully organised and structured stage of existence. In recent years, many long-established local churches have enjoyed a hybrid existence, retaining their links with a historic denomination while establishing supportive and envisioning relationships with a new church network. As new churches become more like denominations, the pressure is likely to increase, from the historic denomination and from the newly adopted network, for the local church to choose definitively a single source of identity, vision and support. This could provoke a new intensification of rivalry in those settings where at present there is a tolerance, if not a comfortable acceptance of the growing number of hybrid churches.

9) Women's ministries

This is a debate that refuses to go away in every denomination. The modern consensus is that the acceptance of women in ministry is a matter of both common sense and justice. Common sense because the gifts required for full-time Christian ministry are not gender specific. Justice because our society is seeking to overturn generations of sexual discrimination. Despite the pressure to restrict the debate to these terms, for evangelicals the central issue is biblical teaching, and in particular the significance of the Pauline letters.

One school centres its understanding on Galatians 3:28, the mandate of radical equality in Christ, contrary to the culture of the Roman Empire and irrespective of gender, race or class. Others centre on 1 Timothy 2:11–15, with its express exclusion of women from teaching and leadership roles. The 'leadership is male' school claims that these prohibitions are universal in application, quite irrespective of cultural context, since they are grounded in the express authority of the apostle who supports his position by making reference to the fall of Eve. At its most extreme, this school recalls the dictum of Henry Ford, who said his customers could have any colour car they wanted, so long as it was black. In some churches, women can fulfil any ministry to which they are called, so long as it is working with children or making the coffee.

The 'leadership is male and female' school argues that, in the first century setting, women were not in a position to teach the Scriptures, since they were usually illiterate. What's more, the only form of religious leadership by women in those days had sexual overtones, notably among the temple prostitutes of the mystery religions. Thus, they argue, while Paul excluded women from certain kinds of leadership on pragmatic, culturally-specific grounds, the Galatian declaration of equality spells out the guiding principle in cultural settings freed from temple prostitution and the almost universal exclusion of women from basic schooling. One problem for the 'inclusives' is to explain Paul's reference to Eve. One problem for the 'exclusives' is to explain, if the issues are as cut and dried as they suggest, how Paul can refer approvingly and without apology to the fact of women exercising a variety of leadership roles in the first churches (for example, Phoebe, the deacon, Romans 16:1; Priscilla, the host of a church and co-teacher of Apollos, Romans 16:3; and Junias, the apostle, Romans 16:7).

Both groups wish to do justice to the Scriptures, but this is an issue where evangelical disagreement has proven intractable. The danger is that the 'inclusives' may dismiss the 'exclusives', treating them with contempt as reactionary chauvinists, in line with the prevailing values of our culture, and so fail to give them credit for a genuine attempt to be faithful to Scripture. Similarly, the 'exclusives' may be tempted to consider themselves the only people who are seeking to be truly biblical and so may all too hastily dismiss their fellow evangelicals as trendy and compromised, unable or unwilling to accept the plain teaching of the Bible.

The policy of evangelical churches will vary enormously for the foreseeable future. Some will open all leadership positions to women, some will open none, and some will open all except that of senior minister. It is to be hoped that these debates will not become increasingly polemical and intense, but rather that we will give due respect to fellow evangelicals who have drawn from the Scriptures conclusions different to our own.

This debate inevitably connects with other thorny issues. The issue of sexual identity and equality is broader than women in full-time ministry. Even those evangelicals who want to retain church leadership as a male preserve defend the broader principle of sexual equality. The medieval idea that only males are created in the image of God has long since been repudiated as biblically indefensible. However, while some are following a trend in our society to speak about equality as persons, without reference to gender, others argue that the biblical perspective is better summed up in the phrase 'equal but different'. That is, we cannot give a full account of a particular individual without taking account of their gender. To some this is common sense; to others, a sexist anathema.

Another related issue is the legitimacy of inclusive, and indeed feminine language and imagery with reference to God. The culture of political correctness has its eyes on the prayer book and the Bible. To be sure, the trend to use inclusive language when speaking of women and men is generally found unexceptionable. But what of references to God? Some biblical references to God are impersonal, some of the most striking metaphors compare God to a mother, and the majority of passages use male analogies. It is beyond dispute that the Judaeo-Christian God is plainly understood to transcend human personality and gender.

Nonetheless, God incarnate in human history became a man, not a woman, and Jesus' own preferred way of referring to God was Abba, Father. Therefore, while it is perfectly appropriate to use the biblical references and metaphors that are not male, most evangelicals will baulk at attempts to 'improve' biblical revelation. To begin the Lord's Prayer with the phrase 'Our father and mother in heaven' is not a refinement but a lamentable distortion of Jesus' prayer. To pray to God as the earth mother is perilously close to embracing feminist neo-paganism. Some speak of the Holy Spirit as the feminine dimension of God alongside God the Father and God the Child (not Son, of course, in the most strictly politically correct circles). This introduces an entirely unwarranted gender specific understanding of the third person of the Trinity with no biblical precedent or justification. As to the banners and icons that celebrate 'Christa', a so-called female Jesus, this practice completely fails to recognise the historical specificity of the incarnation, the crucifixion and the resurrection. These are not merely abstract religious ideas, pinned to a male person as an accident of cultural prejudice. The Christian faith is firmly grounded in the historical Jesus, incarnate, crucified and risen. However well intentioned, these new theologies and liturgies have begun to push beyond the limits of what is recognisable as an authentic expression of orthodox Christian faith. They are in process of becoming a new religion, a matriarchal theism no more than loosely influenced by Jesus Christ and the Trinitarian God revealed in the Christian Bible.

For some evangelicals the debate about the ordination of women has also rekindled an underlying and longstanding controversy about ordination and ministry. Was Milton right to conclude that a presbyter is but a priest writ large? Some fight a rearguard action for the old consensus that the priesthood is intrinsically male. Others are winning the day for an ordained ministry open to both women and men. But a third group of evangelicals continue to insist that we need to recover a more fundamental concern than whether to appoint women to positions of church leadership. That is, when evangelicals will have the courage to call for the final abandonment of 'ordination' altogether, as a post-biblical accretion. For this grouping, the real question is not whether to ordain women, but when we are going to stop ordaining men.

10) Marriage, family and sexuality

Marriage is under attack, the divorce rate continues to escalate and steadily increasing numbers of couples are living together either before or instead of getting married. This raises a number of dilemmas for Christians. How do we affirm the goodness of sex without promoting promiscuity? How do we insist that the only rightful place for sex is within the marriage relationship, without appearing to be prudish and anti-sex? How do we express both the grace of God towards those whose marriages have failed and yet affirm and promote the biblical standard of marriage for life?

The danger is that we affirm grace so strongly that we play down the biblical antagonism to adultery, divorce and casual sexual relationships. Or conversely, that we affirm biblical standards with such hardness that there is no place for forgiveness and a fresh start for those who have experienced the trauma of a failed marriage. It has proven very difficult for the church to combine the two dimensions of Jesus' response to the woman caught in adultery, forgiveness and yet firmness, grace without moral compromise – 'Neither do I condemn you ... Go now and leave your life of sin' (John 8:11).

One thing is clear: our society is neither helped nor taken in by church reports that 'take the sin out of living together'. If we present law without grace, we are perceived to be out of touch and unrealistic. But if the church is seen to be aping the moral standards of our age, courting favour with a secularised generation by selling out on Christian morality, no one is convinced, appeased or won over. When the Church of England produced a notably weak and morally revisionist report in 1995, it was striking that many secular commentators in the national press were the first to pass vigorous comment. Far from applauding the church for finally catching up with the sexual ethics of the sixties, the complaint was almost universal: this is not what we expect or want from the church. Society may not always like or conform to biblical morality, but people are simply not taken in by a numerically shrinking church suddenly abandoning its traditional moral standards and baptising the ethics of the age. To many outsiders, this looks too much like moral cowardice, a desperate effort to look trendy and appealing.

With so many marriages failing, it has become fashionable to denigrate the nuclear family, or at least minimise its social significance. The nuclear family is spoken of as an endangered species, an outmoded human institution. Some look at present trends in society, with the increasing number of single parent families, and warn that to idealise the nuclear family means excluding and marginalising a growing number of homes from authentic experiences of family life, including the unmarried and the divorced as well as single parent families. Others take an historical perspective and point out that pre-industrial concepts of family encompassed the extended family, set in the context of a settled local community. Most people grew up and stayed for life within a single village, in a secure and continuing network of relationships with relatives and friends. In addition, a biblical perspective draws attention to the wider communities in ancient Israel of the tribe and the nation. In the New Testament we can identify further patterns of family and community: the extended households familiar across the Roman Empire; the travelling communities of Jesus' disciples and the apostolic teams; and the family of the local church, where brothers and sisters in Christ met together in their homes. In short, for Christians to put all their eggs into the basket of the nuclear family is to do less than justice to the diverse patterns of family and community in the Bible and in our society, both historically and today.

While family life is, and always has been, more disparate than the specific pattern of the nuclear family, this particular form of home and relationship remains for many in our society both the norm and the ideal. There is no going back to pre-industrial communities, which, after all, were by no means always a utopian idyll. But without that wider framework of relationships, that has presumably been lost forever, the nuclear family is now more isolated than ever before, particularly in the urban setting. The innate human need to belong has become more narrowly focused upon the marriage relationship and the nuclear family, raising the demands that are being made upon our marriages, at a time when marriage itself had become an increasingly fragile and brittle institution. Husband and wife need to look to one another to be not only partner and lover, but also best friend, and co-provider not only of money for the mortgage but also of a sense of belonging in the only community that still exists for many, the micro-community of the home.

While we need to attempt to provide the necessary support and hope for those experiencing other kinds of home life, it is vital that we do not, in reaction against previous over-simplifications, end up marginalising the nuclear family itself. Despite the well-documented crises our society faces in marriage and in family life, many need to be reminded that between 78 and 83 per cent of children under 16 live in the same home as both natural parents, and some 70 per cent of first marriages succeed (statistics quoted in *The Times*, 19 June 1995). In short, the nuclear family is under immense, and perhaps unprecedented pressure, but it still remains the experience and preference of the vast majority. Our society looks to the church not only to support the marginalised, but also to support the family. Now more than ever, nuclear families need help. The nuclear family may not be the only expression of authentic family life, but it is the most common form and the basic building block for community and society. If Christians fail to provide that help, we will contribute not only to the break up of individual families, but also to the accelerating break up of our society.

We turn finally in this group of fracture points to the single issue most likely to bring about the fragmentation of one or more of the historic denominations. The homosexual debate has recently been brought to new prominence, with pro-homosexual lobbyists naming Members of Parliament and bishops whom they claim to be gay. These campaigns are becoming more assertive and their primary targets appear to be the Conservative Party and the Church of England. At the same time, official church reports show a steady liberalising of attitudes, moving towards accepting settled relationships as a kind of 'homosexual marriage' and removing the barriers that have prevented open and practising homosexuals being eligible for ordained ministry.

A prolonged debate continues as to whether homosexual orientation is determined more by heredity, environment or personal choice. When new evidence is introduced into the debate, interpretations of its significance vary enormously. Thus, when geneticists recently reported the possible discovery of a 'gay gene', it provoked entirely contrary reactions. Some pro-gay groups welcomed the possibility, on the grounds that it vindicated homosexual orientation since people were born this way, rather than their orientation being the product of particular and avoidable life experiences. Others were philosophically opposed to the very idea that there could be such a thing as a 'gay gene'. They recognised that if a defective gene could be found, it could then be taken to signify that homosexuality is an aberration from the healthy norm. As a result, medical research would inevitably begin to look for a cure in order to restore normal sexuality. What's more, if it became possible to detect such a gene in the early stages of pregnancy, this would almost certainly lead to the practice of abortion on demand of 'gay foetuses'. These recent controversies demonstrate that, if medical science was able to prove conclusively the existence of a 'gay gene', the implications of such a discovery would remain the focus of enormous dispute.

Five underlying cultural assumptions that fuel the debate about attitudes to homosexuality need to be recognised. First, we live in an age that presumes that a fulfilled life is necessarily sexually active. For many, it would seem absurd to suggest that virginity is to be cherished or that a life without regular sexual activity, such as that of Jesus, could possibly be fulfilled. The second assumption concerns morality. In a climate of relativism, the only widely acceptable moral absolute is that it is indefensible to impose our personal moral values on anyone else. Everyone is granted the liberty to design their own morality and lifestyle. The third assumption is philosophical, arguing that individual identity is a matter of personhood. All references to gender are then treated as anachronistic, even sexist. Philosophical bisexuality therefore argues that all relationships and attractions are a matter of personal choice, arousal and affection. Irrespective of whether those involved happen to be male or female, what matters is that individuals find love together. The fourth assumption makes a connection between sexual orientation and the very essence of personal identity. Thus, while others may define themselves in terms of race, gender, marital status, occupation or personal interests – 'I'm British, male, married with two children, a writer and enjoy rock music' – there is a pressure upon those who publicly acknowledge their homosexuality to perceive themselves expressly and narrowly in sexual terms. Their decisive and essential sense of self is understood to be contained solely and definitively in the statement that they are gay. The fifth assumption is that the only legitimate position for those who consider themselves to be enlightened and just is to set gay relationships on an equal footing with heterosexual relationships. Anyone who opposes this emerging consensus is considered to be a reactionary, a fool or a bigot.

Justice for a persecuted minority is the chosen battleground of the pro-gay groups. It is argued that since homosexuals are naturally predisposed to a particular sexual orientation, they should no longer be made to suffer in the face of prejudices that are a throwback to a previous and ignorant age. This position is well illustrated by the resignation of Paul Boateng MP as a patron of Premier, the London Christian radio station, within days of the station going on air. His concern was the statement of Pete Meadows, the station's chief executive, that Premier would hold to 'the unified view of the Church ... that genital activity between people of the same sex is outside of God's plan and therefore wrong'. In his resignation, the MP did not merely express his strong disagreement with this view, but went on to claim the moral high ground for gay rights. He categorically denounced a policy that did no more than adhere to the traditional moral teaching of the Church as 'totally un-Christian', 'morally repugnant', and 'grotesquely discriminatory'. Richard Kirker, General Secretary of the Lesbian and Gay Christian movement asked for the station's licence to be revoked, on the grounds of a 'blatant attempt to stigmatise and exclude a type of Christian which the station, quite arbitrarily, seems determined to marginalise and reject'. He described the station's policy as 'partisan', 'sectarian' and 'inflammatory'.

The long-standing evangelical response to these issues has been consistent and clear. Evangelicals have renounced homophobia – hatred and persecution of homosexuals. They have affirmed that homosexual orientation is not in itself a sin. But they have insisted that homosexual genital activity, whether casual or in a committed relationship is unacceptable because it is biblically indefensible. If the underlying issue was perceived to be the protection of a persecuted minority some evangelicals would instinctively want to defend the marginalised. But the fundamental issue here is the authority of the Bible. If we develop an interpretation that explains away the clear biblical prohibitions, we will have abandoned our own evangelicalism (Genesis 19:8; Levitius 18:22, 20:13; Judges 19:22–4; Kings 14:24, 15:12, 22:46; Romans 1:26–7, 1 Corinthians 6:9; Jude 7). If we hold fast to biblical morality, we have no choice but to reject the morality of our day. For orthodox evangelicals, practising homosexuals are necessarily living in sin. They cannot be eligible for ordained ministry and they need to repent and change their lifestyle. If present trends continue in several historic denominations, evangelicals may soon be faced with a stark choice: depart with reluctance from a denomination that in its official policy and public statements has fundamentally repudiated biblical morality, or stay put and consequently abandon their evangelical convictions. The storms of controversy that surround this debate are predictable and are likely to escalate and become increadingly acrimonious in the next few years.

11) Annihilationism or eternal punishment
This potential fracture point was given new prominence by John Stott's endorsement of annihilationism in his published dialogue with David Edwards. The debate is both exegetical and theological and continues to divide evangelicals. The literalists note that Jesus teaches about hell more than anyone else in the New Testament, and that his references speak of constant and endless retribution: where the worms never die and the fires never go out. The annihilationists make the objection that eternal punishment seems excessive, and that the manner in which some Christians have dwelt on the fate of the lost is morally repugnant. They argue that Jesus'

descriptions of the last judgment are a series of metaphors derived from the rubbish dump outside the walls of Jerusalem in his day, and therefore cannot be taken as a literal description of an eternal hell. They suggest that the central thrust of Jesus' teaching is that the final judgment is inescapable and final. Those who do not enter into everlasting life will suffer an eternity removed from God's presence, not in the torments of hell, but by being annihilated.

Both evangelical parties reject universalism, on the grounds that final judgment is inescapably taught in the Bible. Neither plays down the reality of human sin or the severity of the consequences. Both give no place to the idea of purgatory, a teaching without any biblical warrant, and both recognise the fact and finality of divine judgment. As a result, both groups will evangelise with the same urgency, because both recognise that our response to Christ in this life will determine our eternal destiny. It is therefore important to note the relative insignificance of this debate, especially since some traditionalists, horrified at the re-emergence of annihilationism among fellow evangelicals, have reacted with a disproportionate vigour that would only be fitting in response to a repudiation of a central and fundamental tenet of the faith.

The debate needs to continue, but with both courtesy and a proper sense of proportion, recognising how much the two parties hold in common. What's more, we need to recognise the extent to which the gruesome extravagance of medieval representations of hell continues to fuel this conflict. Modern distaste at such grisly and macabre excesses will provoke an instinctive move towards annihilationism. At the same time, those convinced that final judgment leads to eternal punishment must be careful not to go beyond the Scriptures, elaborating gory details that in truth have nothing to do with the words of Jesus. A truly evangelical understanding of hell and its occupants should be careful to derive nothing from the fevered imagination behind the nightmare paintings of Hieronymus Bosch. If we must preach hell, we must surely do so without the slightest suggestion of relish, but rather with the deepest sorrow and urgency.

12) Revival and revivalism

Despite the widespread evangelical longing for revival, it is salutary to recall that previous revivals have resulted not only in rapid numerical growth, but also in a measure of evangelical controversy and fragmentation. The secondary manifestations accompanying the Great Awakening led to accusations from the more sedately religious that it was nothing more than a Great Commotion. Urgent preaching of the need to escape from final judgment led to accusations that the evangelists were provoking the masses into an emotional frenzy. The emphatic assertion that regular churchgoing was insufficient to secure salvation led to insinuations that the leaders of revival were in fact destroyers of the traditional church. In short, many loyal churchpeople were opponents of the Great Awakening. What's more, no two revivals have ever been identical, and so all subsequent revivals have been rejected by those evangelicals who are sympathetic in principle to periods of revival, but whose grid for assessing authentic works of God is too rigid to cope with anything unexpected or unprecedented. If a new eruption of spiritual life is not an exact replica of the revival they revere, they conclude all too readily that it cannot possibly be a genuine work of God.

As to 'revivalism', this term refers to those who claim to have developed a universal theory of revival, a mechanism or a series of human actions which are thought to guarantee and necessarily precipitate a revival. The most famous theorist of this kind was Finney. There is no doubt that Finney experienced true revival during his ministry. There is also no doubt that his revivalist methods have consistently failed to produce full revival ever since. Finney's experiences of revival predated his revivalist theories. Although genuine revival appeared to authenticate his well-intended theories, in fact the theories were predicated upon a revival that predated and was not dependent upon the theoretical construct.

This well-intentioned error has not been found only in Finney's teaching. All too often, those engaged in revival develop over-ambitious and over-elaborate theories which claim too much and appear to be authenticated by the events of revival. Meanwhile, those who recognise the inadequacies of the theory all too easily end up going too far. In repudiating the excesses of the theory they may be tempted to write off and repudiate an authentic experience of revival itself. Hyper-Arminians need to accept that true revival requires a crucial factor beyond our control – a sovereign and decisive act of grace in the outpouring of the Spirit of God. Hyper-Calvinists need to accept the fact that Arminians have indeed experienced times of authentic revival, perhaps above all through the ministries of the Wesleys, and not least through the ministry of Finney, notwithstanding the heated controversies his theories have provoked.

13) *Times of refreshing*

1994 saw the outpouring of a major new wave of renewal. Across the denominations and streams, Christians gave countless testimonies about remarkable encounters with the presence and love, holiness and power of the Holy Spirit. The backlash was predictable, and not long in coming. We may categorise the objections into three types: distortions, excesses and contaminations.

As to distortions, evangelicals have always had the highest regard for biblical preaching, and will express concern at any development that appears to diminish the place of preaching. It is perhaps an inevitable consequence that some evangelicals have an exaggerated view of preaching, as if this is the only means of conversion and teaching that God ever uses. Nonetheless, faced with new and eye-catching manifestations of the Holy Spirit's presence and power it must be freely acknowledged that some churches have been too easily diverted from ensuring that preaching is allowed to make its pivotal impact. However, the present period of renewal is by no means anti-preaching, since many leaders and churches have reported a new anointing upon preaching during these times of refreshing.

Considering excesses, we do well to recall Jonathan Edward's warning that great care was needed in periods of intense spiritual activity to prevent the people 'running wild'. Far from making wise and discerning leadership redundant, an outpouring of the Holy Spirit makes it all the more vital, not least in determining those occasions when seeker sensitivity rightly overrides spontaneous freedom of response on the part of believers. Where genuine excesses are discovered, they need to be dealt with promptly. However, we must caution against some common overreactions, provoked by horror stories, the unfamiliar and genuine excess. Horror stories are like the party game of Chinese Whispers – with every retelling the excesses are multiplied. Before passing on such stories, we should always check whether they are based more in exaggeration than fact. We should also be cautious about hasty conclusions provoked by unfamiliar manifestations: just because something does not happen in my church does not automatically guarantee that it cannot be of God! As to genuine excess, it naturally occurs and its chief opponents should always be the keen promoters of a movement. They best cultivate their cause, not by turning a blind eye, but by regular weeding. Genuine excess tends to produce an overreaction in those who are so dismayed that they dig in at the opposite extreme. What's more, no evangelical tribe is without its due measure of concomitant excesses. Accurate evaluation of another tribe begins by identifying their best and lasting strengths. We can never contribute to wise and mature judgements by compiling horror stories from those who have gone over the top and then implying that such disasters typify every participant in the movement we are seeking to attack and discredit. Such an approach is dishonest, manipulative and deliberately divisive.

Turning to the possibility of contamination, fears have been expressed in terms of style, manifestations, theology and evil spirits. There are two distinct styles of ministry predominant in the refreshing. One style is fairly noisy and high octane, and the prayer ministry may be led by a single up-front preacher and be fairly intense. Although some Pentecostals find it hard to recognise themselves in such a description, other Christians would tend to label this a neo-Pentecostal style. For some churches and personality types, it takes a lot of adjustment to cope with such excitability. However, this is by no means the only style, since there are also found within the refreshing other meetings and churches where the ministry style is very laid back, with no hype or pressure at all. Some would characterise this as a Vineyard style of ministry.

Faced with unusual and dramatic manifestations, some critics list similar phenomena in non-Christian groups, whether ancient religions or new age. This is not a new critique for it was used by Charles Chauncy, Jonathan Edward's leading American opponent, to attempt to discredit the Great Awakening. We need to insist that the mere presence of external manifestations cannot in itself prove that the Holy Spirit is at work. Equally, we need to insist that the outbreak of such manifestations cannot possibly prove that we are not encountering an authentic work of God. The biblical and historical case for unusual manifestations is very strong. There is not one manifestation reported from May 1994 onwards that is without precedent in periods of genuine revival or preparation for revival. The decisive tests of authenticity are whether Jesus is glorified and whether there is subsequent growth in holy living.

As to theological concerns, some have suggested that the entire spiritual refreshing is dependent on prosperity teaching. This is a sweeping and shallow misrepresentation. First, the Toronto church, where it all began in the English-speaking world, is a Vineyard church, and John Wimber has developed a network of churches that is not founded on prosperity teaching. Second, while the Toronto leaders were influenced by those with roots in prosperity and faith groupings, they also sought prayer from leaders in the Argentinean Revival. Indeed, the entire movement might better be known as the Argentinean Blessing.

The most decisive factor is simply this: in Britain the refreshing has spread entirely without dependence on any kind of theological package deal. No one has taken out a Toronto franchise, marketing a pre-packaged Canadian theology, let alone a surreptitiously pre-packaged prosperity theology. Not only have those involved not abandoned their existing evangelical convictions, but we have also seen churches embrace the refreshing in historic denominations and new churches, among Arminians and Calvinists, indeed right across the board of the existing spectrum of evangelical convictions. There is no evidence of theological contamination because there has simply been no theological package deal at all.

Finally we turn to the concern that there could be some kind of spiritual contamination. It has been claimed that if a Christian who has been spiritually contaminated lays hands on you, the spirit within them also gains mastery over you. Some elaborate the theory by suggesting that this malignant spiritual virus spreads automatically, wherever there is laying on of hands, not merely direct from the original 'source' person, but through all subsequent contaminants, even though they may have no idea that they have become 'carriers'. Thus, we need to be concerned not only about the orthodoxy and 'spiritual correctness' of anyone who has ever prayed for us, but also the 'spiritual correctness' of everyone who have ever prayed for them. Taken to its logical conclusion, we should never allow anyone to pray for us without first undertaking

an exhaustive check of their 'spiritual family tree', and then repeat
the exercise for everyone who had ever prayed for them, and of
course for everyone who had ever prayed for them, *ad infinitum*.
To be absolutely secure, the research would have to be exhaustive,
and would no doubt require the assistance of a massive computer-
ised database.

What can be said of this spiritual theory? The nearest contemporary parallel is with the transmission of Aids – countless people
becoming carriers through unprotected contact with others who
are already contaminated without any obvious external signs. It
represents a way of thinking that is more McCarthyite than
biblical. For those predisposed to spiritual paranoia such claims
provoke acute anxiety – what if I have ever been prayed for by
someone who was prayed for by someone who was prayed for by
someone who was spiritually contaminated? Such an approach
constructs nothing less than a demonic equivalent of the Catholic
concept of the apostolic succession: to pass it on always requires
the right pair of hands. The very suggestion is deeply dualistic,
suggesting that Satan is more than a match for God. The almost
blasphemous suggestion is that Christians who faithfully pray to
the Father in the name of Jesus for more of the Spirit, are instead
receiving a satanic impartation. Such teaching has no place in
authentic evangelicalism. In an attempt to discredit fellow evangelicals this approach employs sub-Christian scare tactics, malicious
and hysterical, specious and absurd.

When a movement like the present refreshing emerges, there are
two distinct needs. On the one hand, evangelicals of all kinds – the
keen participants, the sympathetic observers, the cautious and the
wary – need to assert as great a measure of unity as possible. We
need to establish a framework for continuing dialogue and also
need to resist the divisive impact of intemperate polemicists who
can emerge from all sides. The Evangelical Alliance sponsored a
24-hour consultation in December 1994 that began this task
admirably for the present refreshing. The agreed statement is found
in Appendix 1. At the same time, those within such a movement
have a complementary but distinct and equally critical task. They
need to provide a constructive lead that seeks not only to provide
vision and direction, but also to ensure that potentially divisive
enthusiasts do not lose sight of the unchanging evangelical foun-

dations that we all hold in common. Evangelicals must never lose sight of the fact that in both our convictions and our actions we hold fast to both the unchanging authority of the Word of God and the unchanging power of the Holy Spirit.

Unity in diversity

As we face up to these fracture points, some fundamental questions arise. How important are our evangelical convictions compared with denominational or other Christian loyalties? What can we legitimately treat as secondary and an inappropriate basis for public dispute and separation? When we must disagree with fellow evangelicals, how do we disagree agreeably? In later chapters we will attempt to develop a response to these pressing concerns.

There is enough explosive stored up in this catalogue of controversies to make the eagerly anticipated firework displays being planned to celebrate the year 2000 look like a bargain basement bonfire night. Faced with such thorny and irretractable differences, it is critical for evangelicals to ensure, while never failing to guard the gospel, that we make every effort to avoid constant and destructive polarisation. Any one of these fracture points has the potential to blow apart the evangelical movement and consensus, unless we are firmly resolved that our greater concern is the preservation and strengthening of evangelical unity and influence, in both society and the church.

6

Evangelical convictions

In the previous chapter we explored many fracture points that could divide evangelicals from one another, but now we need to ask some fundamental questions. What is an evangelical? What convictions are the basis of sustained evangelical unity? Following Bebbington's brilliant analysis of the history of evangelicalism in Britain, it has become customary to identify four key dimensions of evangelical identity: crucicentric, biblicist, conversionist and activist.

The four classical dimensions

i) The centrality of the cross
We are crucicentric, that is cross-centred, because the whole of salvation flows from the cross. It is the pivot of human history, the ultimate source of hope in a world consumed by godlessness and greed. The gospels themselves are cross-centred. Whereas a typical biography will pass over a great person's death in relatively few pages, naturally giving most space and attention to the times of his greatest achievements, as much as one third of the chapters of each gospel is given over to Jesus' last week in Jerusalem.

Just as the gospels centre on Jesus' death as the climax and completion of his ministry on earth, the preaching of the first apostles returned persistently to the cross. Luke's summaries of their preaching make this absolutely plain. For example, Peter's Pentecost sermon comes to a climax around Jesus' death and resurrection: 'God has made this Jesus, whom you crucified, both Lord and Christ' (Acts 2:36). When hauled before the Sanhedrin, he explains the apostles' refusal to keep silent in terms of irrepressible enthusiasm for what God has accomplished before their eyes: 'It is by the name of Jesus Christ of Nazareth, whom you crucified but whom God raised from the dead, that this man stands before you healed' (Acts 4:10). Faced with an unexpected opportunity to witness to Gentiles in Cornelius' household, once again the cross takes centre stage: 'They killed him by hanging him on a tree, but God raised him from the dead on the third day ...' (Acts 10:39–40). Even so, when Paul describes his own preaching ministry, he presents himself as tirelessly returning to a single theme: 'For I was resolved to know nothing while I was with you except Jesus Christ and him crucified' (1 Corinthians 2:2).

The first Christians were by no means crucicentric solely in their preaching. Not surprisingly, we find the same central focus to the apostle's doctrine. Supremely in Paul's letter to the Romans, but also throughout the New Testament, we find clear and thorough exposition of the objectivity of the atonement, explaining the necessity, the sufficiency, the eternal significance and the triumph of the cross. At the cross, grace is revealed, sacrificial love is demonstrated, wrath is appeased, the demands of divine justice are met, the sacrifice of atonement is made, the price for sin is paid, the righteousness from God is made available, the power of sin is defeated, the dominion of death is conquered, and a public spectacle is made of the demonic powers and authorities (eg Romans 3:21–6; 5–8). More than by any other theme, the New Testament letters are marked, in P. T. Forsyth's memorable phrase, by 'the cruciality of the cross'.

Crucifixion was employed by the Romans to strike terror into the subject races across their empire. It must have seemed astonishing to many that this new religion used as a mark of hope and reverence this symbol of imperial domination, the repellent sign of a cruel, barbarous and bloody execution. This use of the familiar symbol of tyranny and disgrace was nothing less than extraordinary. To onlookers it would have seemed as peculiar as a new religious group today using as their badge of honour the symbol of their founder's execution by the state: a gallows, the hypodermic for a lethal injection or an electric chair.

From the convictions of the first Christians, we derive the cross-centredness that has often caused complaint among other church people. 'With these evangelicals,' one denominational leader complained, 'it's always the cross, the power of the cross and nothing but the cross!' The cross lies at the heart of evangelical doctrine, evangelical preaching, evangelical worship and evangelical witness. The critical moment of human history, the ultimate miracle of divine intervention, decisive for all eternity, took place at this first-century public execution. Our understanding of God's character, our responses to the mystery of suffering, our confidence before the forces of darkness, our insistence on the necessity of personal faith in Christ, all these are derived from the astonishing historical event of the crucified God.

ii) Bible believing

In our devotion to the Bible, evangelicals take their lead from Christ himself. Just as Jesus quotes the Old Testament as the Word of God, we accept the divine inspiration and supreme authority of the Scriptures (eg Matthew 4:4,7,10). In the Old Testament, we find a clear argument for the logical necessity of divine revelation. Since God's thoughts are not our thoughts, and his ways are not our ways, the reality of God cannot be attained by human reasoning alone. The mind of God transcends the limits of human understanding. Therefore, if God is to be known, he must first reveal himself (Isaiah 55:8–11).

The apostles readily endorse Jesus' acceptance of the unique inspiration and definitive authority of the Bible. The Old Testament is quoted in their writings as the Word of God (eg Hebrews 1:5–13; Peter 2:6–8), and so, quite naturally, are the words of Jesus (eg 'You have heard ... but I say ... Matthew 5:21–2, 27–8, 31–2, 33–4, 38–9, 43–4). The Scriptures are described as God-breathed, which emphasises not a particular model of verbal inspiration, but rather the unique revelatory authority of the Bible. As a result, the Scriptures have a unique power to equip a believer for every good work, providing teaching, rebuke, correction and training in righteousness (2 Timothy 3:16–17). Peter's second letter explicitly extends this status of divine revelation to the writings of the New Testament (2 Peter 3:15–16). For the evangelical, therefore, the Bible is not merely another source of revelation or authority. The

Bible has supreme authority, above both reason and tradition, recording the definitive revelation in space and time of the living and trinitarian God.

iii) Conversionist

Evangelicals have always insisted on the absolute necessity of conversion and personal faith. It is not enough to go to church, say prayers or be baptised: every single person needs to be born again (John 3:3). This emphasis is rooted in the ministry of Jesus, for the gospels summarise his preaching as a call to repentance and faith (Matthew 4:17; Mk 1:15). The preaching of the apostles continued this clear emphasis: salvation is not through good or religious works, for we are justified by faith alone (Ephesians 2:8–9). To cite no more than a brief selection of the great principles of salvation, together with just a sample of the biblical references, we are new creations (2 Corinthians 5:17; Galatians 6:15), forgiven every stain of sin (Ephesians 1:7; Colossians 1:14), redeemed through his shed blood from the curse of the law and from our previous empty way of life (Galatians 3:13–14; Ephesians 1:7; 1 Peter 1:18), transferred from darkness to light (Colossians 1:13; 1 Peter 2:9), made right with God, not by human effort, but by personal, saving faith in Christ (Romans 4:23, 5:1). As a result, despite the distaste of some non-evangelical church people, and despite the resistance of the unchurched, especially respectable relativists, evangelicals continue to press the need for personal conversion. Conversations with friends, local church events and national missions will all be characterised by explaining the need for salvation. This call to conversion is by no means an arrogant attempt to impose our own convictions upon others. It is the logical consequence of our conclusion that Jesus Christ is not merely another good or wise religious teacher, but the incarnate Son of God (John 1:14; 1 John 4:2), opening a new and living way to God for all who call upon his name (Hebrews 10:20).

iv) Activist

Jesus' years of public ministry were action packed, as he served and sought to save the lost (Matthew 15:24; Mark 10:45), travelling from town to town, demonstrating and declaring in his healing and preaching ministry the ways and the love of God. In the same way, Jesus' Great Commission gives to every generation of evangelicals a command that cannot be avoided to take responsibility for mission to the world (Matthew 28:18–20). Although prayer has sometimes been neglected in the face of such intense need for action, at its best evangelical activism includes an activism in prayer, as seen in the early Church and in subsequent periods of evangelical vitality and revival around the world.

The great champions of evangelicalism demonstrate this heroic activism: Paul in his tireless journeys around the Gentile world; John Wesley on horseback around Britain; Hudson Taylor spending himself for the sake of the Chinese; Charles Spurgeon preaching ten times a week, while establishing a college for preachers, organising a tremendous number of church plants and establishing social action initiatives for the poor. Our convictions about Christ make evangelicals the busiest of Christians. In every generation, evangelicals have a noble, enduring and enormous task: to serve the needy and to win the world.

Two additional dimensions

v) Christocentric

We can identify two further dimensions of evangelical identity that are both central and essential. The first is Christocentricity. The centrality and Lordship of Christ must surely be the primary basis for both evangelical spirituality and evangelical unity. We pray through and to Jesus Christ. We proclaim salvation and pray for healing and deliverance in his name. Our interpretation of the Scriptures is Jesus centred, for he is the fulfilment of Old Testament prophecies and hopes and the definitive and ultimate self-revelation of God. In our preaching and evangelism, disciple making and worship, we tirelessly return to Jesus: his name and person, his divinity and authority, his completed work and promised return. We want to grow more like him, live for him, and walk in the Spirit who is sent by Jesus and the Father. Some might object that Christocentricity is, strictly speaking, a Christian essential rather than a distinctively evangelical essential. This is plainly true, but devotion to Christ nonetheless remains absolutely fundamental to evangelical identity. Without a central focus upon Jesus Christ, the incarnate Son of God, crucified and risen, there would be no evangelical faith or evangelical distinctiveness at all.

vi) Longing for revival

The second additional factor is to recognise that, historically, evangelicals have set a high value upon revival. It was, after all, in the fires of the Great Awakening that a distinctive evangelical identity grew out of the Reformation and Puritan traditions. This shapes our approach to evangelism, ecclesiology, and pneumatology. Longing for revival shapes our evangelism because, while we must always pour our energy, time and money into creative initiatives in our mission to the world, we pray beyond our own efforts for an outbreak of revival power, in which God's mighty work transcends our greatest efforts.

Longing for revival shapes our theology of the church, because the church is never an end in itself as a religious institution, but rather the servant of the gospel of Christ and the Kingdom of God. In periods of revival, much of our theology and the practice of the church needs to be reinvented: new zeal among believers and a rising tide of new converts makes our existing structures and patterns of church life look at best provisional and at worst obsolete. The new wine calls for new wineskins. The wisest leaders in revival not only preach with passion and power, but, as was demonstrated supremely by John Wesley, must also master the necessary skills to manage and sustain a work of God through organising the believers effectively. As Wesley advised: 'Preach in as many places as you can. Start as many classes as you can. Do not preach without starting new classes.'

The history of revival also shapes our theology of the Spirit, because central to revival is the outpouring of the Holy Spirit in power. In modern evangelicalism, the key distinction in terms of the Spirit has usually been whether we see ourselves as charismatic or non-charismatic evangelicals. Historically, the centrality of revival points us to a far more pressing and underlying issue. Are we wary, indifferent or even hostile to revival, with all the attendant outpourings of the Holy Spirit and dramatic manifestations of the divine presence? Or are we revival's passionate advocates? We may recognise the shortcomings and follies that have often accompanied genuine periods of revival, but do we nonetheless shape our hopes and prayers around the longing that Christ might send the holy fire again?

Losing focus?

A measure of corrosion may be detected at the heart of classical evangelical identity. Just when evangelicals are growing in numbers, we are growing lighter in substance: 'New Evangelical Lite, less Bible, low on evangelism and revival free'.

As to the cross, debates have surfaced in some quarters about the centrality and objectivity of the atonement. Some hold to the classical evangelical conviction that penal substitution is pivotal to our understanding of the cross. Others suggest a more nuanced approach, pointing out that legal framework is merely one of several biblical approaches and accounts of the cross. Christ crucified is not only the propitiatory and expiatory sacrifice, he is also the victor over the demonic hordes and the ultimate revelation and demonstration of the love of God. A third group, however, appear inclined to leave penal substitution on one side, not directly denying it, but reducing to forlorn neglect an understanding of the cross that has always been central to evangelical preaching and spirituality.

The authority of the Bible has been at risk of being relegated in two contrasting ways. The enthusiastic entry of evangelicals into mainline scholarship may sometimes have inadvertently blurred any distinctively evangelical approach to the Bible's inspiration, origins and study. One lecturer confided to me in a private conversation that he could no longer see any essential difference between his way of handling Scripture and that of his liberal colleagues, to whom he felt closer than to the average non-academic evangelical Christian. Earlier this century the borders were clearly drawn, with evangelicals consistently arguing against reconstructions of the sources of the Pentateuch, against the possibility of several contributors to the book of Isaiah, against pseudonymity in the New Testament epistles, and against redactional or midrashic reconstructions of the words of Jesus in the Gospels. Today the consensus has shifted on at least some of these issues, and the lines have become much more blurred as to what constitutes authentic evangelical scholarship.

Meanwhile in the churches, a growing biblical illiteracy can be detected. There has been a widely lamented decline in biblical exposition: in too many churches boring platitudes, entertaining but insubstantial anecdotes or the fireworks of a forceful personality have replaced the right dividing of the word of God (2 Timothy 2:14–15), that is, preaching that faithfully expounds biblical truth on fire. At the same time, we have seen in the last twenty years a prolonged reduction in the sales and use of daily Bible reading notes. Either the people have neither the time nor the appetite to read the Bible anymore, or the publishers of notes have singularly failed to provide adequate and suitable approaches for the late twentieth century.

The primacy of evangelism in the mission of the church has been seriously questioned by some who still lay claim to the name evangelical. They are drifting imperceptibly towards a kind of conversion-free religious social work. Others, in emphasising the fact that the majority of conversions take place over a period of time rather than instantaneously, run the risk of overstating their case. The danger is that we end up so stressing the 'journey into faith' that we fail to preach with clarity and persuasive forcefulness the absolute necessity of coming to faith and the full assurance that is found in becoming a new creation in Christ.

Our traditional activism has been increasingly denigrated, sometimes with good reason by those who have suffered burn out due to inordinate and unrealistic demands imposed upon excessively busy lives. In reaction against the excesses of such driven activism, we have seen in some evangelical circles, not a recovery of a more holistic evangelical spirituality, but a new drift into a Catholic and contemplative spirituality, and even a wholesale repudiation of evangelical activism. Contemplative prayer retreats can be richly rewarding, but there is no need to pay the price of abandoning our evangelical activism. We need to learn to live in the creative dynamic commended by Augustine – *semper agens, semper quietens* – always active, always at rest.

Even the centrality of Christ may be at risk of being diminished. Some, in response to modern pluralism in a multi-faith and relativistic society, play down or hedge with diplomatic qualifications the traditional and biblical emphasis of evangelicals upon 'salvation only in his name'. In over-reaction against pietistic docetism, which was incapable of giving adequate recognition to the true humanity of Christ, others have tended to speak of Christ in ways that seem overly casual and irreverent, even jokey and trivialising. Still others are losing any clear emphasis upon the second coming of Christ, partly in reaction against the detailed millennarian timetables of former generations, but also partly as a result of over-realised eschatology. They concentrate almost entirely upon what God wants to achieve in the here and now, failing to emphasise that some dimensions of salvation will only be completed and fulfilled in the resurrection life to come.

To a greater degree than for many years, revival is returning to the agenda of evangelicals in Britain. The theology of revival will almost certainly rekindle the presently dormant debate between Calvinists and Arminians. Any experience of revival, judging from historical precedents, will very likely lead both to new unity, transcending denominational allegiances and also to new divisions. If we not only restore revival to a prominent place, but actually enter a period of genuine revival, it will play havoc with the present day respectability of our churchmanship. Revival movements which bring many thousands to Christ inevitably bring charges of 'enthusiasm' from respectable denominationalists, who normally find the whole event quite alien and repellent. What's more, some evangelicals will probably reject any modern day revival, disturbed by strong emotional responses and the bizarre physical manifestations that generally accompany such a move of God. Has the price of increasing denominational respectability become a reluctance to speak in favour of revival? Do evangelicals still pray with passion and anticipate with longing a mighty new wave of revival at the end of the twentieth century?

Sources of corrosion

If there is indeed a corrosion of evangelical identity several culprits may be identified. We live in a culture that cherishes relativism as the only absolute. Relativism is a self-contradictory position for it claims that all truth is relative except for the absolute truth that all truth is relative. Despite this fatal logical flaw, relativism has become the dominant perspective on life in our culture today.

Because it has become the habitual way of thinking for many, it consequently appears to be both natural and self-evidently correct. Such a conviction is inimical to all orthodox truth claims about Jesus Christ, the cross and the gospel. But the impact of relativism is not restricted to non-Christians. Because we inhabit the same culture, we are shaped by the same values and presuppositions, particularly because they underlie not only modern popular culture, above all in the mass media, but also the consensus of the liberal, intellectual elite in higher education. As a result, these pervasive values imperceptibly distort the perspective of evangelicals. A powerful pressure is upon us to apologise with embarrassment for our 'quaint and old-fashioned prejudices', rather than declare without compromise the absolute truths of the gospel.

Other factors are derived not from modern culture, but from particular trends within the wider church. Firstly there is the persuasive allure of the diplomacy of preferment. When evangelicals seek to win respectability in their denominations, they may feel obliged to play down those distinctions that are less palatable to non-evangelicals. Some may begin to sound the tune of a 'broad churchman', for fear of missing out on career advancement for being 'too evangelical' and not a 'proper denominationalist'. The fear of being labelled a 'fundamentalist' can make someone bend over backwards to win the approval of non-evangelicals, seeking to demonstrate their breadth of thinking and win broad denominational acceptance. Others move imperceptibly into the mainstream consensus of academic theology, until they cease to be recognisable as evangelicals at all. This is not to decry all participation in denominational hierarchies or academic theology. On the contrary, we need evangelical representation in these circles, and great advances have been made in the last quarter century. But there is a price tag, and there have been instances when it has seemed less likely that our fellow evangelicals will bring evangelical reform than that they will be swallowed whole, assimilated into a fundamental compromise within the non-evangelical status quo.

Biblical illiteracy is both a cause and an effect of this loss of focus in evangelical identity. The commitment to the Bible has been evident in the traditional emphasis upon group Bible studies, personal Bible reading and thoroughly biblical preaching. Where the emphasis upon being a Bible believing Christian has been eroded, the Bible will slip from this prominent position in our meetings and personal lives. Equally, where there is less time for the Bible, less knowledge of biblical teaching is bound to follow. In time, biblically illiterate evangelicals will become less aware of aberrations in doctrine and less alert to continued corrosion in the traditional evangelical distinctions.

One further and common source of corrosion is ignorance of evangelical history. We live in a culture of the now, where all that matters is existential immediacy. Why bother discovering the past, when we can be immersed in a TV soap or a computer game? What's more, many modern evangelicals consider themselves to have escaped from an arid past of dead orthodoxy, deeply tainted by pharisaical legalism. In over-reaction, some behave as if there is nothing left to learn from the past. Whatever the errors and excesses of previous generations of evangelicals, we do well to remind ourselves that our forbears were able to preserve and hand on the gospel, frequently in a theological climate that was hostile to our essential convictions. If we choose to remain ignorant of our past, we may be less able to guard and preserve the gospel in our day, whether against direct and overt theological assaults, or against winsome dilution into a kind of semi-evangelical, or even post-evangelical, neo-orthodoxy.

If we are to recover lost ground and undo the corrosive diminution of our essential evangelical identity, two initiatives need to be considered. Firstly, a new evangelical statement of faith is required for the twenty-first century, a credal restatement of classical evangelical convictions, expressed in terms that will win broad and ready assent around the world. Why a restatement? Because the historic evangelical bases of faith are limited in two ways. Firstly, the language of the statements of faith currently in wide circulation has become dated and therefore steadily more difficult to comprehend. Secondly, some key phrases were strongly influenced by the need to provide an evangelical corrective to the theological debates and the liberal consensus at the time the statement was composed. It is inevitable that these issues will no longer necessarily be the most pressing for present and future generations of evangelicals. What's more, we are seeing the death of liberal theology in the West, at a time when evangelicals are on the march around the world, enjoying an accelerating rate of conversion growth. Now is surely the moment to call for a new, international, evangelical basis of faith.

Alongside this new evangelical creed, we also need to restate and recover our historical identity and priorities, our apostolic centre of gravity:

Evangelicals are Christ-centred, cross-centred and Bible believing;
we stress the necessity of conversion
and the importance of active service in mission for all disciples of
    Christ;
and we eagerly pray for and anticipate a new wave of revival.

7

Evangelical identity

We have argued that it is essential for evangelicals to reappraise present day adherence to classical evangelical convictions. We have also recognised the reefs on which contemporary evangelical unity may be shipwrecked. It is just as important that we re-examine the status and consequences of our evangelical identity. What weight do we attach to the statement that we count ourselves to be evangelicals? Is this a secondary aspect of Christian allegiance, merely one among many of the substrata of spiritual traditions? If so, we will readily come to the conclusion that evangelical identity is of much less weight than our denominational convictions and standing. On the other hand, could it be more precise and appropriate to recognise that evangelicalism is our primary identity? If so, our evangelical identity will transcend the demands and priorities of denominational allegiance.

The twin breeds of evangelical

Within every denomination and stream there are two distinct breeds of evangelical. I am referring to something deeper than the difference between conservatives and radicals or between charismatics and non-charismatics. A still more fundamental distinction needs to be faced. There are evangelicals who also happen to be Anglican, Baptist or whatever. There are also convinced denominationalists who also happen to hold evangelical convictions. These two breeds have a different sense of identity and are shaped by different priorities. As a result, they can easily misunderstand each other.

We can illustrate this contrast in terms of one particular denomination, but similar patterns are found in every sector of church life. The evangelical Baptist prefers to refer someone who is moving to a new area to the nearest live Baptist church. However, the leader who is first an evangelical will refer someone to the nearest live church, irrespective of denomination. The evangelical Baptist will warmly identify with the 'Baptist family'. The Baptist evangelical will identify more readily with the wider evangelical scene than with non-evangelical Baptist Union churches. The evangelical Baptist will be concerned primarily with the need to plant new Baptist churches. The Baptist evangelical will identify first with the wider vision of planting new Bible believing, lively and evangelising churches, irrespective of denominational label.

Denomination first

The evangelical whose first loyalty lies with their denomination will devote their energies to the denomination, whether in terms of giving and prayer or in terms of the events and activities that are promoted and attended. A primary focus upon denomination will also, in subtle but unmistakable ways, establish a pervasive, general and determinative sense of identity and ethos. Although they genuinely appreciate opportunities to mix with fellow evangelicals, this breed of evangelical ultimately feels much more at home with their own denominational kind. Some will frankly acknowledge that they can understand and relate more readily to non-evangelicals within their own denomination than to evangelicals beyond their tribe. What's more, the laudable concern to bring reform within their own denomination may in practice leave very little time available for active involvement in the wider evangelical scene.

This type of evangelical can be found in every denomination. We will illustrate their characteristics from two of the largest groups of evangelicals and two of the fastest growing. For the evangelical Anglican, being an Anglican is absolutely fundamental to how you see yourself as a Christian. It matters a great deal for your church to maintain strong links with other Anglican churches, to support Anglican missionary societies, to play a full part in diocesan and synodical life, and to relate to churches overseas within the Anglican communion. In short, for the evangelical Anglican, being an Anglican comes first. As a result, Anglican initiatives, whether broadly denominational or specifically evangelical, will always tend to take centre stage. Among some Anglicans, who remain the largest single group of evangelicals, this kind of approach has sometimes resulted in what looks to non-Anglicans like a go-it-alone strategy, putting energy mainly into their own denomination and into evangelical activities that are denominationally specific. The result has been a measure of detachment from the wider evangelical world. What's more, in a class-ridden society, denominations still reflect to some degree the various social strata from which they derive their origins. Non-Anglican evangelicals still claim to detect from time to time the unmistakable intimations of an Oxbridge aroma of presumed social and intellectual superiority.

Among Baptists, the second largest group of evangelicals, some exhibit a similar heightened sense of denominational consciousness and priorities, together with a similar exclusiveness, clearly indicating their prior loyalty to the specifically Baptist cause. More frequent are those Baptists profoundly influenced by a distinctive and almost anti-denominational tradition of hyper-independency. It is not that they have little time for wider evangelical networks because they are so heavily committed to denominational activities. Rather, they tend to operate at all times in splendid (or, in truth decidedly less than splendid) isolation! They cut themselves off from denominational and wider evangelical participation alike.

Among Pentecostals, a history of sustained marginalisation by fellow evangelicals can lead to an inherited wariness of others. Having coped for the best part of a century with being ostracised, ignored, and treated as the Cinderellas of the evangelical world, it is only natural that some will continue to feel like outsiders, still preferring to keep to their own kind today. Some Pentecostals explain that this instinctive and traditional isolation is reinforced by continuing anti-Pentecostal bias among other evangelicals. For example, one leading Pentecostal suggested to me that when well known international speakers visit Britain, and they come from a 'respectable historic denomination', their denominational credentials will usually be declared, often with a measure of pride on the part of those from the same denominational tribe. However, when the visiting speakers are Pentecostal, their denominational allegiance is more likely to go unmentioned when they speak at a pan-evangelical event. Whether or not this perception is accurate, it plainly indicates that some Pentecostals still feel marginalised by their fellow evangelicals in Britain today.

As for the new churches, some have shown a clear resolve to overcome separatism, proving themselves to be more than willing to work with those in historic and theologically-mixed denominations. Indeed many recent pan-evangelical initiatives have arisen from this stable. However, this inclusive evangelical co-operation can nonetheless sometimes be accompanied by an underlying assumption that their own churches are where the real action is to be found. The youthful dynamism of a movement, just as much as the venerable age of an institution, can lead to pride and exclusivism. Wherever there is an underlying presumption of superiority, in whatever denomination or stream, however politely concealed and no matter how much co-operation is commended, evangelical co-operation is bound, in practice, to prove a restricted and secondary concern.

Evangelicals first

For those who are evangelicals first, what matters most is not their particular denominational setting but rather their grounding upon evangelical bedrock. Their primary sense of identity and conviction is evangelical, not denominational. Their denominational identity therefore serves as an adjective, describing their particular expression of evangelical convictions. The growth and strength of evangelicalism is ultimately of more concern than the growth and strength of the denomination. As a result, it matters a great deal for the local church to establish strong links with other like-minded, evangelical churches in the area, irrespective of their various denominations or streams. What's more, those who see themselves primarily as evangelicals want to support a wide range of evangelical mission agencies, rather than putting all their eggs into a denominational basket.

Those for whom evangelical convictions come first have sometimes been accused of having an inadequate, or indeed almost non-existent, doctrine of the church. For example, I was converted and called to full-time ministry in an Anglican setting, and some leaders I met in those days made no attempt to disguise the fact that their involvement in the Anglican church was a matter of pragmatism. They were not Anglicans because of doctrinal conviction, but because of access to non-Christians. 'I'm an Anglican,' they would explain, 'because it's the best boat to fish from!' Such a view of denominational ecclesiology has naturally led others to have little sympathy with evangelicals who have been viewed as semi-detached from the heartlands of denominational life.

Denominational loyalty – paying the price?

The last few years have been notable for the emergence of two extremely contrasting, not to say polar opposite, trends among evangelicals – renascent denominationalism and post-denominationalism. On the one hand, facing up to the inadequacy of the pragmatism described above, some evangelical leaders have become steadily more emphatic and definite in their denominational convictions. At its worst, this can result in a newly entrenched and ardent denominationalist practically unchurching everyone who does not belong to his or her particular denominational fold. Indeed, at a consultation of evangelicals in the historic denominations a few years ago, one senior Anglican took such a line towards all the Free Churches, old and new alike. While I enjoyed taking him on head to head in the ensuing public debate, I was all the more pleased that those who objected most strenuously to his position included many of his fellow Anglicans.

Emphatic denominational loyalty can lead not only to detachment from fellow evangelicals, but also to watering down evangelical convictions. At the height of David Jenkins' notoriety, the Bishop of Durham seemed guaranteed to steal the headlines at major Christian festivals with further expressions of radical scepticism. The press loved his ability to shock the British public: here was a senior bishop who appeared to believe less of the gospel than the average British non-churchgoer. Ironically, his public parading of professorial doubts led to much airtime being given to evangelical convictions, since prominent evangelicals were frequently invited to debate with him in the media.

Evangelicals are not totalitarian: any theologian is entitled to express his or her opinions, just as we are entitled in turn to give a robust and considered defence of orthodoxy. However, many of us, including some Anglican evangelicals, were unable to see how it could be appropriate, or even legitimate, for a man of such convictions to become a senior bishop. His beliefs, or lack of them, seemed to make a nonsense of the vows he made at his enthronement to defend the orthodox faith.

It was therefore striking and regrettable to discover that some of the unbelieving bishop's most strenuous supporters were found among some evangelical Anglicans, defending their co-religionist and distancing themselves from those evangelicals who found it necessary to contradict his pronouncements. Some went so far as to suggest that his agnosticism was advantageous to the gospel, helping the unchurched to bring their doubts into the open, and to discover they had more in common with the church than they might have supposed. Such tortuous logic reminds me of the story of the sceptic and the churchgoer. 'I am as much a Christian as you are!' the sceptic asserted. When the churchgoer asked for an explanation, he received this reply. 'I don't believe in the virgin birth and nor do you. I don't believe in the bodily resurrection of Christ and nor do you. I don't believe in the Second Coming and the final judgment, and nor do you. Therefore, since you believe no more than I do, I have just as much right to call myself a Christian as you do!'

The gospel task given to Timothy by Paul remains the duty of every generation of Christian leaders: to guard the gospel against every kind of diminution or dilution, contamination or compromise. There is no excuse for our guardianship being less than polite, courteous and gracious. But our duty and resolve must never be shaken to guard the eternal and unchanging truths of the good news of Jesus Christ.

Denominational reform – a case study

Despite the hazards that have sometimes ensnared us, we can assert with confidence that the evangelical recovery of genuine, active and thoroughgoing commitment to denominational participation has resulted in major gains across several denominations, not only in terms of evangelicals being appointed to high office, but also in the restatement of biblical ethics and orthodox doctrine together with a renewed denominational commitment to evangelism and church planting.

One of the most significant examples in recent years of denominational engagement and reform is in the influence of Mainstream grouping within the Baptist Union. A small denomination in Britain, Baptists are one of the largest Protestant denominations in the world, and in many countries Baptists are seeing significant growth. British Baptists have usually been thought of as a mainly evangelical denomination. This is reflected in the large Baptist attendance at Spring Harvest, and their high level of participation in national evangelistic campaigns. Both historically and today Baptists are essentially not a broad church but rather an evangelical movement.

Growth hasn't always happened. In fact it is only comparatively recently that we can speak of an evangelical resurgence. For many years the denomination was drifting from its roots, just as Spurgeon had warned would happen, and Baptists faced the same sorry decline as other churches through most of this century. The late sixties and early seventies were for many a spiritual dark age. Alongside continued numerical shrinkage there was a decline into radically unbiblical theology and, in some quarters, an intolerance towards evangelical convictions.

Looking back, the seventies proved the decisive turning point. In 1972 radical questioning of the divinity of Christ was raised by a senior liberal Baptist, not in a theological seminar but in a main meeting of the Baptist Union Assembly. For some this was the last straw. Over 40 churches and ministers abandoned ship, resigning their denominational membership. Others were convinced that they should seek reform and renewal within the denomination. Pat Goodland, one of the key figures in this group, recalls that their meetings and prayers were 'born out of a deep sense of concern at our churches' lack of life and growth'.

In 1977, the annual report of the Baptist Union spoke of continued decline in the tones of resignation, even defeatism. At the annual assembly Douglas McBain could contain himself no longer. Many recall his impassioned plea for urgent analysis and prayer, which was speedily re-affirmed by Paul Beasley-Murray when he scented prevarication from the assembly chairman. Times have changed for these young turks of evangelicalism who assailed the establishment. Douglas is now area superintendent for London; Paul went on to serve as principal of Spurgeon's College.

By the end of the seventies, a major new grouping for evangelical Baptists had been formed. Mainstream has never had a formal membership, but provides a regular newsletter, an annual conference since 1980, and the occasional preaching workshop or theological consultation. There have never been Mainstream issues or Mainstream candidates for senior posts, but Mainstream quickly became a rallying point for Baptist evangelicals. What's more, the movement's slogans have emphatically embraced mission as central to living orthodoxy – Baptists for life and growth; a Word and Spirit network. At first Mainstream was dismissed. Some disregarded it as tiny and irrelevant, others slammed it as divisive and fundamentalist, or accused the leaders of being 'charismatic confectioners'. Despite such dismissive attitudes, the name had been chosen well. This was no minor tributary but expressed the evangelical convictions that have always been central to Baptist churches, sustaining and motivating them in their life and mission. Throughout the eighties and into the nineties, a ground swell of local church leaders readily endorsed the Mainstream vision.

Evangelical vigour is not only seen in national conferences and local growth. Recent years have seen a steady and increasing flow of evangelical appointments to senior denominational positions, many of them active supporters and participants in Mainstream. David Coffey, a well known Spring Harvest speaker, was made national secretary for evangelism, and even before he took office many evangelicals found fresh inspiration from his appointment. Then, in Spring 1991, he was appointed general secretary of the Baptist Union. Meanwhile, Derek Tidball, now principal of London Bible College, was elected Baptist Union president and was then appointed as Baptist Union secretary for mission and evangelism. Both David and Derek had previously served on the Mainstream executive, David as secretary and Derek as chair.

The tide is flowing among evangelicals training for ministry, since most of the trainee Baptist ministers are evangelicals. A recent college survey showed that most are also positively influenced by renewal. More surprising, in the light of severe staff shortages in other denominations, is the fact that the numbers applying for training have kept growing. Alongside a sustained level of applications for college places, recent years have seen new approaches to training. Most colleges have now developed in-pastorate training as an alternative to college-based courses. Probably even more significant is the development at Spurgeon's of specialised training for church-based evangelists and church planters.

There is no room for complacency. Present growth is an encouraging beginning, but nowhere near enough! Local churches and national leaders alike are calling for a decisive shift of priority from maintenance (keeping Christians comfortable) to mission (reaching a lost world). Mainstream have therefore strongly supported attempts to establish a national mission strategy and have warmly supported calls for a national numerical target for new church plants this decade.

At every level – numerical growth, senior appointments, increasing numbers of trained leaders, an ambitious evangelistic strategy – the evidence is clear. We are witnessing an evangelical resurgence among Baptists unprecedented this century. Despite these promising reforms and developments, Baptists would lose out if they became isolated from other Christians. All of us need to learn from each other. What's more, the nation can only be reached if all evangelicals work together. Derek Tidball sums up the new climate of expectancy – 'We're part of that new tide of the Spirit sweeping across the nation, and across the denominations.'

To be sure, Baptists are a very different breed to the other historic denominations, being much less of a broad church. Methodists and United Reformed evangelicals may look ruefully towards a denomination where evangelicals are in the overwhelming majority, when in their own setting the evangelical minority

sometimes feel beleaguered, misrepresented or even ignored.
Nonetheless, it is only as a result of active and sustained participation within the denominational structures that such successes of
evangelical recovery and reform have been achieved. Those whose
only contribution to denominational life is to snipe from the
sidelines doom themselves to a marginalised future.

Post-denominationalism

We have been exploring both the gains and hazards of resurgent
denominational participation among evangelicals. Among full-
time leaders and clergy, evangelical engagement and thoroughgoing participation in denominational structures has undoubtedly
been the dominant trend of the last twenty years. With not a little
irony, in many congregations the very opposite trend has simul-
taneously emerged. The people are becoming increasingly reluctant to identify themselves lifelong according to a particular
denominational label. Instead they have become interdenominational migrants. When they move home, growing numbers of
Christians look for a nearby church that is biblical and lively, with
an almost complete disregard for denomination. Partly this is due
to increasing mobility: the more times people move, the more
likely that they will end up living in a place where there is no live
church representing their original denomination. Partly it is due
to the success of events like Spring Harvest, where Christians are
exposed to the best evangelical speakers in a setting where their
denominational identity is secondary, and for many even irrelevant. Partly this semi-detachment from old style denominational
loyalties reflects a cultural shift, where younger generations are
increasingly reluctant to sign up to any institution for life, preferring a relational and provisional kind of participation. It certainly
also reflects the inability of at least some denominations to market
themselves attractively and convincingly to post-war generations:
all too often denominational events and literature can seem stuffy,
outmoded and irrelevant.

For many contemporary Christians, advances in evangelical
influence at denominational level leave them cold. It's on another
planet, no more than obliquely related to their own life, worship

and witness. Temporary, provisional involvement has replaced lifetime loyalty. An invitation to subscribe to a denominational paper can be met with incomprehension – 'Why on earth should I?' The suggestion that a denominational gathering might be a genuine alternative to a lively evangelical conference or Bible week is met with incredulity – 'Why should I go there? I don't belong to any denomination. I simply belong to our local church.'

This new and advancing wave of post-denominationalism is a bitter pill for many ministers and denominational leaders to swallow. Just when they are making real inroads of evangelical influence and reform in their denomination, a growing number of the people decide that they no longer care for denominations at all. The most denominationally-minded Christians are often in full-time ministry. They have invested the most into their denominational setting. This is not only a matter of having worked through their own ecclesiology more thoroughly. Many have invested time and energy into denominational committees and reports. Many have little exposure to the Sunday services and church life of other denominations. Moreover, of all Christians they are the least likely to be denominational nomads, usually locked into a particular church not only theologically but also in terms of identity, housing, and even their pension plan.

It is not surprising that some denominationalists agonise over the dilution of denominational identity and draw up new programmes to educate Christians into lifelong loyalty to their particular tribe. But the people are ahead of the game. They have discovered the liberty of being able to say 'I am a Christian, and I go to a live church in my area.' Declining to accept a denominational label has not impaired their Christian witness or identity. Rather, they have discovered a new freedom. Structural ecumenism concentrates on helping august religious institutions talk to one another. Grass roots evangelical ecumenism cuts out the 'middle men' in the denominational structures, as the people choose to celebrate the reality of their unity as Bible believing Christians. Once this liberation has been tasted, whatever the reservations of some ministers, there is no turning back. Post-denominationalism is an idea whose time has come. Increasing numbers of Christians are handing in their old denominational identities and becoming free agents in the Kingdom of God.

Evangelicals together

Though we could pursue similar studies of growing influence and reform in denomination after denomination, we turn now to an equally fine example of evangelical advance in a non-denominational setting, namely the resurgence of the Evangelical Alliance. The figures for personal and church membership speak for themselves, showing sustained growth over several years, to the point where evangelicals now comprise once again the majority of Protestants in the United Kingdom.

Just as evangelicals influence their denomination by active participation, when we take a stand together with fellow evangelicals we can influence the nation. Since evangelicals are the only growing sector of the church in Britain, and since we now represent the majority of Protestants, we have become a force to be reckoned with, a body of opinion to be taken seriously. The *Independent* has described evangelicals as 'on the march', while the *Daily Telegraph* has concluded that we 'are now a force for social change – far more powerful than many of their critics realize'. As the *Sunday Times* expressed it, 'This much seems beyond doubt: the future is theirs.'

As the number of evangelicals has grown to the present figure of 1.25 million, the increase in the membership of the Evangelical Alliance has been followed closely by the increasing number of invitations to senior evangelicals to speak out in the press, on radio and on television. The sheer number of evangelicals means that the director general of the Evangelical Alliance is considered by secular journalists to be a more newsworthy spokesman than the leaders of the small denominations. Evangelical leaders in the denominations need never be threatened by such developments, for the increasing prominence of the Evangelical Alliance is surely a sign of hope. It is a new-minted demonstration of a long-recognised truth: there is more we can achieve together than apart.

The limits of evangelical co-operation

At a recent symposium of evangelical leaders, one minister expressed the aspiration that the day would not be far off when churches would identify themselves not by denomination but as evangelical churches. For the reasons we have examined in this chapter, some gave glad assent to this hope, while others were clearly less comfortable. Since the EA staff need to continue to serve both types of evangelical, there were signs of a certain awkward embarrassment among them. In the light of such aspirations, which are guaranteed to stir evangelicals both to hope and to horror, it is necessary to recognise the limits of evangelical co-operation.

There is no agreed evangelical ecclesiology. In part this is the direct result of evangelical concentration upon evangelism – with such an emphasis it is hardly surprising that the doctrine of the church has usually remained a Cinderella beside the doctrine of salvation. What's more, not only do many historic denominations substantially pre-date the Evangelical alliance, but evangelicals today generally join together having already entered into denominational allegiances. Our evangelical unity has therefore always had to work around existing commitments to divergent patterns of church government and organisation. In short, a denomination is one thing that the Evangelical Alliance not only is not, but could not possibly become. It is in fact a logical impossibility. Far from having an agreed evangelical ecclesiology, this is one of the areas in which we have consistently agreed to differ. There is no likelihood whatsoever that evangelicals would be able to agree unanimously upon the construction of a single pattern of evangelical church. On the contrary, the Alliance is best seen as a pan-evangelical coalition, within which the various kinds of evangelical can work in partnership together. That is not to exclude the possibility of churches identifying themselves as evangelical churches before all else. Nor can we exclude the possibility of a re-alignment of some evangelicals into new denominations or quasi-denominational groupings. But the Evangelical Alliance itself has neither the desire nor the remotest possibility of becoming an evangelical denomination. It is an entirely different kind of organisation. Our various kinds of churchmanship set limits upon our co-operation, even as our common evangelical convictions keep us together.

Mutual recognition

Due to differences of background and temperament that lead to either cautious or adventurous inclinations, at least as much as divergent theological convictions, neither denominational evangelicals nor evangelical denominationalists are a breed facing the prospect of extinction. However, each group has the ability to make life uncomfortable for the other.

Those who are primarily evangelicals can lapse into cynicism about denominational involvement. I have been sorry to hear someone dismissed as a 'company man', or held under suspicion as an establishment figure, within months of taking up a senior denominational appointment. We need to rejoice in the fact that, as a result of the evangelical resurgence of the last quarter century, many evangelicals are serving with integrity within the corridors of their denominational edifice.

The evangelical denominationalist can become equally strident, urging everyone to get involved in the committees which seem to plague denominational life: such a task is surely a special calling from which some strategic leaders, whether teachers, visionaries or evangelists, need to be preserved at all costs! I have been sorry to hear someone dismissed as 'disloyal' or even held in suspicion as a covert anti-denominationalist, when they are serving with integrity within the networks of wider evangelicalism. Some leaders readily have the grace to recognise that others have a different calling from their own. Others evidently find it more difficult to conceive that some leaders have a different calling and therefore different priorities, as equally valid as their own.

What can we make of these distinctions? It must be healthy, first of all to face squarely the diversity between these two breeds of evangelical. We must resist the tendency to squeeze everyone into a single mould or approach, and repent of any misplaced judgmentalism or peer pressure towards shallow conformity. We need to promote a greater degree of mutual respect for callings and perspectives which, while significantly different to one another, need never be seen as mutually exclusive. Instead of trying to turn everyone into a denominational evangelical or everyone into an evangelical denominationalist, it's about time we accepted a simple truth: we will certainly not always agree, but, for the sake of the gospel of Christ, the more we learn to respect and trust one another, the stronger we will be.

The primary identity

While I want to argue for the necessity of renewed sense of mutual respect and understanding, there is still a fundamental question to ask about our evangelical identity. Just how important are our evangelical convictions? Do they supplement our foundational beliefs and denominational identity? Or are they primary, the bedrock upon which all else needs to be built?

If we are to establish a clear hierarchy of identities, we must begin by stating the obvious. First and fundamentally we are *Christians*. All other distinctive emphases are necessarily subordinate to personal faith in Christ. Without living faith, all other convictions, whether denominational or theological, will prove ultimately impotent. We are saved by faith in Christ alone.

Directly derived from our response to Christ is submission to the Bible, for Jesus plainly demonstrated in his handling of Scripture that these writings should be reverenced and submitted to as nothing less than the revealed Word of God. Following Christ's example, the apostles taught the first Christians to accept the Old Testament and also the writings that became the New Testament as the sacred texts of divine revelation, and so our submission to Scriptural authority demonstrates our adherence to the apostolic teaching and faith. The supreme authority of the Scriptures is therefore the foundation on which we build all subsequent doctrinal and ethical convictions. Far from being a secondary or incidental characteristic, to speak of ourselves as evangelical is surely foundational, to be declared without apology or defensiveness alongside the name Christian as the most significant statement about our convictions and identity as followers of Christ. To be an evangelical is to be a Christian who holds unreservedly to the apostolic faith.

For myself, I would then add two adjectives to the name

evangelical: charismatic and reformed. The former describes a particular understanding of the work of the Holy Spirit and the free availability of all the spiritual gifts today. The latter describes a particular understanding of God's sovereignty and grace. Other evangelicals might describe themselves as non-charismatic or as Arminian. In both cases, while I consider my own convictions to be derived from my evangelical identity, I nonetheless recognise that other evangelicals have drawn different conclusions. Therefore these convictions must be considered sub-sets of evangelicalism. Since evangelicals have not reached unanimity over these issues, it would be unrealistic and inappropriate to claim that specific and detailed agreement is necessary for us to be able to make any legitimate claim to the name evangelical.

As to the denominational identity, this should surely be treated in a similar way, of substantially less significance than our evangelical convictions. Indeed, when examined carefully, even our denominational identity can be sub-divided into several categories. To take myself as an example, in terms of *formative influences*, I was shaped by the Anglican churches where I was converted, filled with the Spirit and called to full-time ministry. In terms of *settled personal conviction*, I have become a Free Churchman and committed to believers' baptism. In terms of *active participation*, I have trained and served as a Baptist minister, and am now serving in a New Frontiers Church that has retained its Baptist roots.

We have argued that, however much or little we see ourselves as active participants in denominational life and reform, whether fully engaged or semi-detached, we need to understand, respect and support one another. More than that, we need to recognise the logical and theological priority of our evangelical identity. Our settled conviction surely needs to be not to see ourselves first as an Anglican, a Baptist, a Pentecostal or a Methodist. Before all else, we are evangelical Christians.

8

Together for Truth

... Suddenly the ball was at his feet, he passed it across the goalmouth, and the striker crashed it into the back of the net! Selhurst Park erupted with delight. Crowds of standing, cheering fans saluted their heroes. It was a goal, and ripples of euphoria spread through a crowd intoxicated with the heady joy of success. Kick-off again, and the tumult began to subside. An interval of mid-field play reduced the noise level still further. Then as the tannoy of the loudspeaker system crackled into life the crowd exploded once more. Yet nothing of note was happening on the field of play to cause the commotion!

I and two of my children are ardent fans of Wimbledon Football Club. I enjoy watching football, find the atmosphere exhilarating, and appreciate skilful play. What I find hard to stomach is the roar of appreciation whenever the loudspeaker announces that Crystal Palace is losing – the noise is nearly as raucous as when we score ourselves!

The problem lies in the fact that Wimbledon F. C. and Crystal Palace are near neighbours and share the Palace ground. Local rivalry is intense and many supporters share a mutual loathing of each other's team. While this may appear to be a natural reaction it takes partisan support one step further than I would wish. It should be possible to support a team without denigrating another. Football can be enjoyed whoever is playing – while success for one's own club just adds icing to the cake. Distaste and disapproval can then be reserved for foul-play, time wasting, bribery and those who refuse to play by the rules of the game. For lovers of good football have more to unite than divide them – whichever team is playing!

Divided we stand

The twentieth century has proved a time of great turmoil for evangelical Christians in the United Kingdom. Confronted by the assaults of liberal theology and popular unbelief we have retreated into our church buildings and hidden away, protecting both ourselves and the message which Jesus has given us to proclaim. Occasionally we have re-emerged from our ghettoes, often focusing around a particular outreach or mission, in order to throw mortar bombs at the enemy! This withdrawal into the isolation of our 'evangelical ghettoes' has often resulted in fighting internal battles rather than external ones. Frequently we have been so obsessed with the particular stance or emphasis of our own church or fellowship that we have neglected to take the good news of Jesus to others. It has become easier to denounce the style, practices and perceived excesses of other evangelicals than to confront the scepticism of our modern world. Consequently much evangelical conversation has concentrated upon issues like the ordination of women, the Toronto Blessing or the manner of the Second Coming of Christ. Issues such as theism, agnosticism, postmodernism, relativism and the rejection of Christian beliefs by society at large have been left largely unanswered.

As evangelicals we have to recognise the scandal of our own divisions. We need to face the challenge of a watching world. We must acknowledge our Lord's desire that we should 'go and make disciples of all nations' (Matthew 28:19). Then, if our lack of unity gets in the way of this, we must ask how we can find a proper basis for mutual understanding and support of each other – despite our differences.

This same aspiration lay close to the heart of Jesus himself. He insisted that his people should be 'one'. This would be the means for the world to recognise who he is, and that his message was true.

To a world which continually demands a miracle, or at least a sign, Jesus left the greatest wonder of all. Not simply a healing, the spontaneous feeding of the crowds, the subjugation of the storm to his will, or even the wonder of his resurrection. Instead he repeated himself as he prayed in the garden. His ultimate desire, expressed four times in the intimacy of conversation with his father, was that his people might be one (John 17:11, 21–3).

This concern for the united witness of his people was not limited to the disciples, but to all who would come after them as followers of Jesus. This unity was then to provide the most perfect illustration of the way in which Jesus is united with his Father. It would prove twin truths to those in a watching world prepared to recognise the truth. That Jesus really is the Son of God, and despite all its imperfections the church possesses the glorious status of being Jesus' body on earth and his bride-to-be in heaven (John 17:22–3). In this repeated request Jesus articulated his will, his specific intention for his church. His own wish was that old and young, rich and poor, employers and employees, male and female, black and white – his Church – might be united together.

The desire of Jesus was therefore for the church to represent the one place in society where there was to be no racial discrimination, class-preference, generation gap, or any other form of division. This was to be the greatest miracle of all. A society of all different kinds of people, yet bonded together in loving commitment as one body, because they loved Jesus.[1]

Together in recent history

This should provide the most perfect foundation for our presentation of the message of Jesus. The main problem is that so often our divisions can get in the way and obscure the truth.

It was only at the beginning of the nineteenth century that Anglicans and Nonconformists first began to co-operate directly together in the mission of the Church. Nonconformists had felt the pressure of discrimination against them in areas of university entrance, Parliamentary participation, education and burying their dead. Added to this was the forcible payment of a church rate to the very Anglican establishment which they regarded as their oppressor. Anglicans saw their Nonconformist counterparts as schismatics who usually lacked qualifications and provided unnecessary competition to their ministry.

For half a century from the establishment of the Bible Society in 1804 patient efforts saw new co-operation emerge in overseas mission, Bible translation and tract distribution. This development continued with the establishment of the London City Mission in the 1830s and other united efforts in evangelism were soon to follow.

Anglicans and non-Anglicans worked together, or along parallel lines, in several areas of social and philanthropic concern. The erection of orphanages, the initiatives for the reduction of working hours for women and children, the introduction of schemes to support the disabled, and the movement for the abolition of slavery were all indicative of effective evangelical social action.

Several campaigns were sponsored by the Evangelical Alliance in the attempt to curb the violation of human rights and to alleviate conditions of religious persecution in various parts of the world. The combination of the Congregationalist, James Davis; the Baptist, Edward Steane; the Lutheran, Hermann Schmettau, and the Anglican, Lord Ebury, indicated the common concern and constructive partnership which could be produced by pan-evangelical co-operation.

The work of American revivalists like Charles Finney, James Caughey and Phoebe Palmer, connected with 'holiness' movements, contributed to the birth of the historic Keswick Convention in 1875. Here, for the first time, evangelicals from all major denominations united together in worship and ministry annually.

The interdenominational evangelistic campaigns associated with Dwight L. Moody and his soloist Ira D. Sankey heralded the dawn of a new era in evangelical co-operation. The 1901 united mission in London, and other visits from international evangelists continued the trend. Yet after a young Youth for Christ evangelist, named Billy Graham, arrived in post-war Britain in 1946 evangelism in the United Kingdom would never be quite the same again.

The Evangelical Alliance brought Billy Graham to Harringay Arena in 1954 and the mission had to be doubled in length by popular demand. His subsequent visits in 1955, 1961, 1966 and 1967 culminated in one million people attending his Mission England in 1984. Further visits since then have continued to demonstrate the appeal of his forthright evangelical preaching. No single individual in the last two hundred years has provided a greater focus for united evangelical activity than Billy Graham. Yet he avoided restricting his mission to evangelicals, any church could participate. His theory was simple, he would not adapt his message or compromise his challenge in any way – so churches could choose whether they wished to join in, or not. As Gavin Reid, now Bishop of Maidstone, but then national director of Mission England, has said, 'What we tried to do was to put our plans on the table in view of all and say frankly that we had no intention of losing control of the project or changing the theological assumptions.'[2] Such open-handedness would not usually be possible, evangelicals have traditionally required greater safeguards. But Billy Graham has acquired such stature and reputation that he has welcomed all to hear his message and never adjusted it to accommodate their theology.

The nineteenth-century missionary movement witnessed an enormous expansion in the spread of the gospel worldwide. It spawned a vast number of new interdenominational missionary societies as diverse as the Qua Iboe Mission (1887), the Mission to Lepers (1874) and the China Inland Mission (1865) to name but a few. Despite innumerable instances of persecution, deprivation, hardship and death, missionary pioneers of all denominations carried the gospel to far-off lands and transformed Christianity into an actual worldwide faith.

This example of co-operation has been translated during the twentieth century into a burgeoning host of parachurch societies. These are involved in diverse areas of mission, evangelism and social concern and provide the focus for pan-evangelical co-operation from those of every denomination. Most parachurch bodies operate on the basis of an agreed statement of faith in order to preserve their evangelical identity and prevent intrusion from a variety of sects and cults which operate in the United Kingdom.

The metamorphosis that has taken place in just two centuries has transformed the evangelical world. Parachurch societies, missionary groups and evangelistic campaigns all offer diverse opportunities for partnership unprecedented in previous centuries. Denominational loyalty and transdenominational partnership have proved unlikely bed-fellows, but have unique opportunities to co-exist together.

Together – but divided

It is possible for this willingness to work together to be over-estimated. The picture of evangelical homogeneity portrayed by some secular commentators can prove to be far from the mark. For calls to the visible unity of evangelicals, sharing together in a single evangelical church are usually ignored.

In 1966, Dr Martyn Lloyd-Jones called, in his famous address at the National Assembly of Evangelicals, for evangelicals to separate themselves from denominations in which they were joined by non-evangelicals. Despite the enormous prestige of 'the Doctor', and the esteem in which he was held, he was largely rebuffed. Evangelicals have generally chosen to divide themselves from each other according to their preference for a form of worship, a style of church government and particular doctrinal emphases, rather than attempt to join directly as one church and attempt to accommodate all their differences. One would not normally see those who disagree with the practice of 'speaking in tongues' worshipping in a Pentecostal church. Nor would one see those who look for a spontaneous form of worship participating regularly in the more rigid framework of a 'hymn-prayer sandwich'.

One surprising facet of evangelical life in the 1980s and 1990s has been the erosion of denominational allegiance. A by-product of both ecumenism and the growing sense of evangelical transferral of commitment between churches. This is particularly true when an individual who moves from one location to another is faced with the question of which church to attend.

No longer will someone attending an Anglican church in one place automatically join another Anglican church in their new area. Other factors will come into play. These will include the style of worship, the content of preaching and the focus of ministry. This does not reflect denominational disenchantment but rather a developing pragmatism towards church attendance.

Someone who attended an evangelical Anglican church in one area is far more likely to select an evangelical church or fellowship of another denomination if the local Anglican church is non-evangelical.

This has not resulted in the rejection of denominations by evangelicals. These are normally viewed as a necessary part of the ecclesiastical framework. Many evangelicals are wholehearted in their involvement within denominational structures, but what is normally rejected is a spirit of denominationalism. What this has meant is that the old division of evangelicals according to their denominational affiliation is no longer as relevant as it once was. Today we have to recognise that evangelicals possess a greater sense of shared identity and can be regarded as one people, but separated into different tribes.

It is not an easy task to classify the diverse streams of evangelical Christianity which survive alongside each other in the UK church today. One attempt has suggested the existence of twelve tribes in this way:

1. Anglican evangelicals
About one in four who attend the Church of England are evangelicals. Their focus is in the Anglican Evangelical Assembly and the Church of England Evangelical Council. Many are linked to the Church Pastoral Aid Society and Church Society.

2. Pentecostals
The three largest Pentecostal denominations are the Assemblies of God, Elim and the Apostolic Churches.

3. Ethnic churches
A major force are the so-called 'black churches' of African or Caribbean origin. Mainly Pentecostal, they include an extensive number of denominations and churches in association with each other. The largest denomination is the New Testament Church of God. There are also many other ethnic churches in Britain including Asian, Chinese, Spanish, Portuguese and Iranian.

4. Renewal groupings
Charismatic evangelicals are a significant sub-section in all denominations. Some have their own identity, as with Anglican renewal ministries in the Church of England. According to the English

Church Census, around 7,000 English Roman Catholics would see themselves as 'charismatic' or 'evangelical'.

5. Separatists
These are mainly reformed (Calvinist) in their theology. They are not willing to be part of a denomination that includes non-evangelicals. Some also separate from evangelicals who are part of such mixed denominations. Key groups of separatist evangelicals include the Evangelical Movement of Wales, the Free Church of Scotland, the Grace Baptists and the British Evangelical Council.

6. Reformed evangelicals
Evangelicals of reformed (Calvinist) persuasion exist within major denominations. For example, the (Anglican) Church Society and, more recently, the Proclamation Trust, and the Reform Group.

7. Evangelical majorities
These are those in a denomination where the vast majority are evangelicals. This includes the Salvation Army, the Presbyterian Church of Ireland and the Baptist Union.

8. Evangelical minorities
Some evangelicals are part of denominations where they are in the minority. This includes the Methodist Church, the Congregational Union and the United Reformed Church. Several have their own organisations within the denomination to foster their identity and objectives. These include 'Headway' in Methodism and the Group for Evangelism And Renewal (GEAR) in the URC.

9. Evangelical non-denominational groups
These are independent churches that are loosely affiliated, but denying denominational structure or identity. Wholly evangelical, these include the Christian Brethren, the Assembly of God churches and churches within the Fellowship of Independent Evangelical Churches.

10. The New Churches
The title 'New Churches' has replaced the ineptly named 'House Church Movement'. In the main, these are groups of churches linked under the leadership of someone they regard as an apostle.

11. *Independents*
Many evangelicals are in churches which maintain a total independence, but are often happy to co-operate with fellow evangelicals elsewhere.

12. *Evangelical denominations*
Some small denominations are totally evangelical – including the Free Church of England, the Churches of Christ and the Independent Methodists.[3]

Together in mission

Confronted by the reality of such diversity one may be tempted to ask on what grounds evangelicals might ever be prepared to submerge their differences in order to work together. The answer lies in the area of mission and evangelism, for evangelicals have always been more concerned about the spread of the Christian message than any other single issue.

Partnership in this task has emerged at a more visible level, and with greater frequency in recent years. This is largely because, despite internal disagreements, evangelicals possess a common mind in four critical areas:

(i) The need for personal conversion: evangelicals are united in the conviction that a follower of Christ is a person who has undergone a miraculous and fundamental change of nature (2 Corinthians 5:17). While a time and place may not necessarily be put on this experience, such a transformation is not achieved by personal religious effort. It is the result of a supernatural work of God in the life of an individual.

Evangelicals are committed to a gospel that turns people, in repentance and faith, from sin to God. This saving faith is a gift from God which can be received on the basis of Christ's death on the cross. A person who receives the gift of salvation is brought into a new relationship with God as their Father – in other words, they have been converted!

(ii) The need to actively demonstrate the reality of saving faith: this will be seen in a desire to witness, pray and live in such a way that others will be drawn to commit their lives to Jesus Christ.

This emphasis on lifestyle is not confined to evangelism. After years of non-involvement British evangelicals have begun to return to their nineteenth-century roots of social action. Evangelical para-church societies like CARE, Shaftesbury Society and Frontier Youth Trust have pioneered a renewal in evangelical social concern. Local churches have also begun to gain a growing commitment to community involvement. This has not taken place at the expense of evangelism. Instead, social involvement apart from evangelism is increasingly regarded as little more than 'spiritual humanism' – while evangelism apart from caring community involvement has come to be seen as merely 'words without deeds'.

The results have been seen in a growing involvement in personal witness and evangelistic initiatives, alongside fresh opportunities for making evangelical perspectives on national issues known in the corridors of power.

Evangelicals have been concerned to act as 'salt and light' (Matthew 5:13) in national society and local community alike. Their theology is one of action and could be summarised in the conclusion that, 'Good deeds will not save a person, but a person who is saved will show it by their good deeds'.

(iii) The need to affirm that the Bible is the Word of God: evangelical Christians are united in seeking to proclaim a biblical gospel. They regard Scripture as the 'final court of appeal' in any issue of behaviour or belief.

This attitude was summarised by John Stott in these words, 'We evangelicals are Bible people ... We believe that Scripture is precisely the written speech of God, and that because it is God's word it has supreme authority over the Church. The supremacy of Scripture has always been and will always be the first hallmark of an evangelical.'[4]

This should not mean that evangelicals reject serious biblical study and debate. Although a few groupings within the overall evangelical community remain suspicious concerning biblical scholarship, the vast majority believe that the integrity of God's truth can survive human investigation. It is acknowledged that when evangelical scholars engage in proper academic scholarship the arguments of sceptics can be refuted and the Bible's message become more clearly understood and seriously applied to the condition of today's world.

For evangelicals Scripture is to be treated with reverence, not out of superstition, but as providing a unique revelation of the character and will of God.

(iv) The need to recognise that the cross of Christ lies at the heart of true faith: it was John Wesley, the founder of Methodism, who pointed out that, 'Nothing in the Christian System (ie teaching) is of greater consequence than the Doctrine of the Atonement'.[5] This vital concept of the reconciliation of people to God, by the means of Christ's death on the cross, has always been central to evangelical belief. The cross is never to be seen as a tragic mistake, but rather as the fulfilment of God's essential plan to redeem a people to himself. Only through Christ's death, by taking our place on the cross, could salvation be achieved, without the cross we would be without hope, and without God, alone in this world.

These four factors unite evangelicals in their Christian witness. We are conversionist, activist, biblicist and crucicentristic in our belief, it is precisely this that makes us evangelicals.[6] On this ground co-operation in evangelism has become possible – and for many it is regarded as vital.

Although evangelical churches are enjoying growth there is an increasing recognition of the size of the task that confronts them. When viewed in terms of evangelism and social action, the inevitable conclusion has been drawn that so much remains to be done.

When our gaze wanders overseas the challenge becomes even greater. It has been recognised that working together offers a more authoritative voice within secular society, and that more can be achieved through partnership than a solo or independent initiative.

It has been observed that, 'When local churches stop living as isolated congregations and link up with others, their united resources can create projects big enough to break into the mega community. There comes a time when the editors have to admit that we are news.'[7]

In Coventry there are between 60 and 70 churches working together on a series of evangelistic initiatives such as 'Christ in the precinct', which takes place during Holy Week. In 1989 they were able to transmit evangelistic programmes from six churches by cable TV, directly into people's homes. This was only achieved because the churches' united strength gave them the evidence required to claim that they represented a large minority group in the area.

Similarly, in 1994, the local council in the Essex seaside resort of Frinton-on-Sea refused permission for the erection of a marquee on the beach. This was to be the focal point of a children's mission. It took the combined weight of the Methodists, Free Church, Anglican, Roman Catholic and Plymouth Brethren churches to persuade the council to change its decision so that the mission could go ahead.

Recent national projects like 'On Fire', March for Jesus, From Minus to Plus and the JIM initiative all began from individual tribes but then gained greater prominence by enlisting wider evangelical support. Many of these initiatives have, of course, moved beyond traditional evangelical roots to a broad ecumenical framework, while retaining their wholehearted commitment to an evangelical message. This has come from their reluctance to exclude any who wish to share in evangelistic outreach, while still being concerned to safeguard the integrity of the evangelical gospel they proclaim. Inevitably, some problems have then resulted over the issue of which church new believers should then be placed in.

Broadly speaking co-operation in evangelism and mission continues to increase with fewer churches acting as if they are the only true church in the neighbourhood. More and more churches are recognising that they can achieve more together providing that there is unanimity over the basis of the message they will share.

As church planting increases churches can still feel slighted by the intrusion of a new neighbour. Vision needs to increase in order that competitiveness diminish and the universal Church increase. Dr Neil Summerton has expressed a view that is increasingly being expressed by local church leaders: 'Churches need to work together at the local level to encourage and strengthen one another in growth and planting.'[8] In other words we need each other.

Together for the future?

Since the middle of the twentieth century evangelicalism has undergone a remarkable resurgence around the world. This has been particularly marked in Britain.

At a time when social observers of religious trends were predicting an era of terminal decline, evangelicals were experiencing remarkable growth. Some churches were numbering attenders in several hundreds and around 30 could claim a membership of about a thousand. The flagship among these is the Elim Pentecostal Kensington Temple which now numbers its congregation in thousands.

This is all a far cry from the early years of the century when evangelicals appeared to be a small, almost moribund, tiny minority. In the unflattering words of Bishop Hensley Henson it was 'an army of illiterates generaled by octogenarians'.[9] This is certainly not the situation which prevails today.

One informed contemporary verdict insists that, 'In Britain evangelicalism has become a movement of enormous strength'. Boasting well in excess of one million adherents, evangelicals can point to growth in every major denomination, noticeably including those that are experiencing general decline.

Evangelicals have now assumed major positions in national church and parachurch leadership. Their voice has become increasingly significant in ecumenical and denominational debates. While Anglican theological colleges now record the fact that over 50 per cent of their ordinands come from an evangelical tradition.

Greater involvement in national Government, television and radio, community associations, education, medicine, the financial world and local politics serves to enhance the image that evangelicalism is alive and well in Britain today. The English Church Census of 1989 reinforced this picture with the conclusions of its extensive analysis affirming that one-third of the churches, and 43 per cent of Protestant churchgoers, would call themselves 'evangelical'.

This same impression is repeated worldwide, for evangelicalism is a global phenomenon. In Costa Rica the number of evangelical churches doubled in only four years. The USA has witnessed an evangelical renewal within the mainline denominations, and the take-over of many denominational institutions by evangelicals.[10] The strongly Roman Catholic country of Brazil is now witnessing a change in its ecclesiastical and theological ethos. Brazil now has around 25,000,000 evangelicals, easily outnumbering all of those in Western Europe. In 1900 in Latin America there were only some 50,000 evangelicals. Today's estimate is over 130,000,000. Worldwide evangelicals now number approximately 300,000,000 people.

Meanwhile in the United Kingdom over 50 per cent of Anglican ordinands are evangelicals, TEAR Fund (The Evangelical Alliance Relief Fund) has risen to become the twenty-fifth largest charity in Great Britain, and Spring Harvest draws some 80,000 evangelicals together every Easter for its teaching weeks and celebrations.[11]

Evangelicals can readily assume that their future looks bright. One of the finest examples of a new crop of evangelical theologians, Alister McGrath, looks at an evangelicalism which was threatened with extinction just decades ago, but is now marked by evangelistic success and a growing intellectual presence to conclude, 'The future seems to beckon for evangelicalism'.[12] That same sense of hope is confirmed by a *Sunday Times* correspondent who commented that, as far as evangelicals are concerned, 'The future belongs to them'.

However, it would be both facile and unrealistic to pretend that all is going well. While optimism prevails there remain some serious objections that confront the cause of evangelical unity. As one leading evangelical has remarked, 'Evangelicals have the ball at their feet. It remains to be seen if they can avoid the temptation of putting it into their own net.'

It is important to recognise that despite so many positive factors all is not well with evangelical unity. Divisions over the 'Toronto Blessing' have only highlighted what many have suspected for a long time, that evangelicals would concentrate on unity while they were declining, when growth came it would be accompanied by the danger of fragmentation. Ian Coffey has wisely commented on this self-destructive trend, 'One of the lessons of history is that when evangelicals are weak they make attempts to group with others who share their outlook. Conversely, when they are strong they tend to pull apart.'[13]

If evangelicals are to face their future together adequately then three serious issues will need to be addressed.

(i) Ecumenism

This is a point at which evangelicals have traditionally disagreed with each other. While two-thirds of British evangelicals belong to denominations that are linked with the ecumenical process, one-third do not.

Careful consideration will have to be given as to where evangelicals can work with Catholics and liberals, and where they cannot. For to blindly co-operate without safeguards could result in a loss of evangelical identity. Equally, to accept only those who wear our badge may be to exclude others among whom the Holy Spirit is at work.

Adopting a *via media*, while avoiding compromise will not be an easy task. For 'separated' evangelicals will continue to insist, along with Alan Gibson, that, 'there is also a duty for churches to bear witness to the gospel, not only by their preaching but also by the company they keep'.[14]

This is a vexed issue, but some attitudes are softening. The fact remains that evangelicals are recovering a sense of unity rather than of union. They are willing to work together on the basis of shared convictions rather than seeking to gain agreement on every issue. If this continues it may well outlast schemes for church 'union'.

(ii) Evangelical Alliance

This body was established by 915 leaders at an international conference in London as long ago as 1846. The Alliance was created to act as a visible focus for evangelical unity and plays a significant role in enabling evangelicals to maintain a dialogue with each other.

The growth of the EA in the last two decades has owed much to the developing desire for unity among evangelicals. Dr Derek Tidball in a generous analysis concludes that, 'The Evangelical Alliance has become a movement to be reckoned with. Justifiably claiming to represent one million evangelicals, it has adopted a pro-active stance and is now widely consulted by the Government and even more widely by the media in a way previously unknown, at least in its recent history. Intervention has borne fruit in the area of Sunday trading, commercial advertising, religious TV, issues of religious liberty and a host of others.'[15]

In its 150th anniversary year it has been said by many that 'if the Evangelical Alliance did not exist we should have to invent it'. Whether it is the Alliance, or a new body, a table on which the pieces of the evangelical jigsaw can be put together remains a crucial factor in the progress of evangelical unity.

(iii) Over-confidence

Evangelicals have always exhibited the tendency to suggest that all is going well. The sense of pride and arrogance that this denotes could herald a fall far more spectacular than their rise!

For all is not always right with evangelicalism. It has a darker side which is focused around an innate sense of dogmatism. This is best defined as a refusal to allow disagreement or doubt. Yet evangelicals do have disagreements about the intransigence of much evangelical opinion, its sub-culture legalism, and imperviousness to much of the pain and uncertainty extant in society today.

Evangelicals do also possess doubts, and these are too often unhelpfully suppressed. John Calvin insisted that, 'when we stress that faith ought to be certain and secure, we do not have in mind a certainty without doubt, or a security without anxiety'. We would do well to learn the pastoral implications of this, because sometimes an intrinsic uncertainty will leave evangelicals majoring on minor issues.

Too often the sense of insecurity, coming from a reluctance to explore the heart of our faith honestly and confront the assaults made upon it, will leave us blowing up less fundamental issues between ourselves. This will only force evangelicals to defend themselves to each other when they should be unitedly proclaiming the gospel to the world.

If the words of Jesus about our intrinsic unity are to be accepted by evangelicals, then we need to put them into practice. For it is only as we co-operate together, support and love each other, that contemporary society will ever recognise the truth of the message we proclaim. It is the demonstration of the reality we proclaim that our world is unconsciously waiting to see. At that point our message becomes the explanation of our lifestyle, not an excuse for the absence of an observable difference in our relationships together.

In a survey commissioned by the then Bishop of Coventry, Rt Revd Cuthbert Bardsley, those outside the church were asked what changes they most wanted to see in the lives of practising Christians. The replies highlighted three areas – a more casual attitude to material possessions, a less sombre view of life and a greater sense of mutual togetherness.

The sober fact is that distinctives of class, gender and race, the absence of obvious personal trust and respect, and the pervasive presence of sectarian attitudes can seriously prejudice the effectiveness of our Christian witness today.

It can be argued that currently evangelicals stand at a significant crossroads of opportunity. The road ahead forks in two opposite directions. One fork points towards the kind of fragmentation that is produced by a 'let's go it alone' mentality, which Protestants have proved themselves to be uniquely adept at producing. Breakaway groups form over secondary issues, disputes emerge over the minutest point of doctrinal interpretation, disagreements take place over methodology, and personality clashes emerge between strong leaders.

The other fork points towards the expansion of evangelism and mission borne out of pan-evangelical co-operation. This recognises that unity does not mean uniformity, and that legitimate differences are not only permissible but actually strengthen our mission – provided that an unambiguous commitment to the essentials of Christian faith is maintained.

Wise leaders seek unity, ambitious people thrive on making their reputations through divinity. History alone will show which road evangelicals may choose to take.

9

Disagreement and evangelical unity

The history of evangelicalism tells us that among those with strong convictions a recurring pattern of debate and disagreement is inevitable. Among contemporary evangelicals, the long-established tradition of vigorous disagreement, with non-Christians, non-evangelical church people and also with fellow evangelicals, has increasingly fallen into disrepute. Some are distancing themselves from former dogmatic and polemical attitudes in a conscious embrace of an ecumenical understanding of John 17. Others have to put much effort into pursuing a relational priority, building networks based on friendships among all who profess love for Christ, irrespective of denomination. Some highly relational evangelicals look with distaste at any kind of dispute, just as others still appear to relish every opportunity for high octane theological knockabout. Are evangelicals disputatious by nature? Is there something about our convictions that makes us peculiarly prone to fractious attitudes and divisions? Or is our proneness to disagreement an unwanted disposition or accretion that needs to be evicted, once for all?

The habit of disagreeing badly

To disagree badly is easy, for we only need to do what comes naturally. All too often, our disagreements are marked by hasty judgements. Defenders of the faith fall prey to conclusions that are premature and all too categorical, and to public judgments that are intemperate and excessive. Edicts are issued with an *ex cathedra* authority, and swallowed whole by faithful followers. Once someone has gone into print with a definitive statement, a full or even partial retraction is difficult to secure.

For several centuries the preferred Western method for engaging in theological, or indeed many other kinds of dispute, has been through pamphlets. The only guaranteed beneficiaries of such theological combat were, of course, the publishers of the leading controversialists. Today, while pamphleteering is a relatively neglected form of communication and dispute, the two favoured approaches are more brief, and therefore even more prone to simplification and sloganeering. For communication among Christians, those involved in a dispute may circulate a newsletter to their followers which may include sweeping generalisations, without any right to reply. For communication beyond their own supporters, the fax-based dispute is just coming into its own. In recent years, Christian leaders have begun to experience a new kind of lobbying, a barrage via the fax machine. Though this can become oppressive, and even risk paralysing an understaffed office with limited phone lines, there is a still worse way of handling disagreements by fax: going direct to the secular press with press releases. The fax machine encourages running to the media. The opportunity to circulate an almost instantaneous press release gives the impression that if a response is delayed, the newsworthy moment may be lost for ever. As a result, the temptation is to treat the fax machine like a verbal machine gun, firing off responses without first consulting other Christians. In the next decade, no doubt, e-mail and the Internet will increasingly become an influential forum for such off-the-cuff judgements and instant responses, evaluations and critiques.

In the heat of the moment, faxes despatched in rapid fire response can result in a double failure. We neglect to make ourselves accountable to our friends and supporters, who may conclude that the speed, content or tone of our reaction is unwise. We also risk the even more serious omission of failing to consult in private those with whom we dispute in public. As a result, we all too easily misrepresent an individual's convictions or distort a Christian movement by making colourful generalisations not based upon what is typical but upon the excesses of a minority who have gone over the top. I have frequently met leaders who are entirely unable to recognise their own convictions or the public meetings they have sponsored from the caricatures painted by fellow Christians. When we encounter horror stories, they should be kept discreetly under wraps and checked at source. It should be left entirely to the gossip columns of the gutter press to make a hasty public parade out of rumour, innuendo and knee-jerk responses.

Unspoken differences

If we probe beneath the surface of many disagreements, we often discover one or more of the following underlying differences and tensions. Firstly, the different tribes of evangelicals hold quite different convictions on secondary issues. If these come to the fore, any disagreement is likely to intensify. Secondly, there may be unspoken rivalries, provoked by similarities of ministry or even by contrasting social and educational backgrounds. Pride and jealousy are sins of the heart that exact a terrible toll if they are not regularly purged from the system. Occasionally someone appears to make a career move out of intemperate denunciation of fellow evangelicals, a ministry grounded not in grace but in negative assertions. If it's not reds under the beds, it's false teaching behind innumerable prominent Christian leaders. For a little while they may make a name for themselves and become the centre of attention, the wise person who can unfailingly unmask all error. Eventually, however, others grow tired of their quasi-McCarthyite conspiracy theories. Thirdly, personality clashes will arise. Leaders of genuine godliness and integrity may sometimes find it extremely difficult to understand one another or cope with one another's style of ministry, let alone agree or co-operate effectively. Fourthly, someone's disproportionate public denunciations may indicate a hidden personal crisis of disappointment or wounding. The cynic is often a disappointed idealist, who can see no good in the aspirations or actions of those who still hold the dreams he once held dear. If someone close to you has been the casualty of another evangelical's mishandling, it is all too easy to become the staunchest critic of anything remotely connected with that person, tarring with the same brush many who would not wish to be associated with the behaviour or teaching that caused the problem in the first place. An individual's trauma can be the spur to a polemic that is bitter and unyielding.

In addition to all these underlying dynamics, there is the potentially immense impact of generational rivalries. What seems a natural style or method to older leaders, will often appear hopelessly dated to younger generations. What's more, some older leaders will feel threatened by the emergence and increasing prominence of leaders who are young enough to be their children. At the same time, ambitious young leaders may become impatient with the inertia among their seniors that continues to bolster the status quo. When new generations of leaders feel starved of opportunity, their frustration will easily boil over in intemperate and sweeping denunciations of the caution and predictability, the boring and outmoded approaches of the 'old guard'. For the sake of evangelical co-operation and the sustained advance of the gospel, those who hold power need to work deliberately and persistently to give power away. They need to release opportunities to younger leaders and help them to grow in experience and wisdom as quickly as possible. At the same time, younger leaders need to ensure that they continually renounce the ageist prejudices which dominate our divided culture. All too quickly, today's young Turks become tomorrow's old guard.

The necessity of disagreement

While some disagreements are nothing more than a distraction, and in some disagreements the protagonists have undoubtedly lost all sense of proportion, there is nonetheless an evangelical responsibility to protect and contend for the gospel. The apostolic responsibility that Paul conferred upon Timothy was not only to pass on the original message faithfully, but also to guard Christian orthodoxy against contamination from any source, whether attack from those beyond the church or from distortion by professing Christians (2 Timothy 1:3–14, 2:2).

Paul was not imposing upon Timothy a principle ignored in his own ministry. The Pauline letters regularly address errors of doctrine and practice. Indeed, where Paul came across behaviour that was inappropriate, it seems to have been his custom to enquire whether it had been caused by some underlying theological error. Distorted doctrine almost inevitably leads to a contaminated lifestyle. Despite the risk that we may appear to be contentious merely by custom or temperament, the apostolic example demonstrates, for all who are dedicated to being defenders of the faith, the necessity of being prepared to disagree with vigour. Therefore, while we recognise the unconscious motivations that have surely distorted, exaggerated and prolonged many Christian disputes, we cannot avoid the obligation to be prepared to fight for the faith, contending anew for the gospel in our generation.

The art of disagreeing well

It is one thing to disagree and quite another to disagree well. An evangelical approach to the art of effective disagreement must begin with the teaching of Jesus about church discipline (Matthew 18:15–17). Step one is the private consultation, bringing a fellow Christian's error to their attention face to face. The clear implication is that it is quite inappropriate to discuss such faults with others behind the back of the offending party. Any public denunciation is still more uncalled for at this initial stage. In addition, while the intention is to bring the other party to repentance, those who bring the criticism must naturally be prepared to apologise if their understanding of the problem proves to be mistaken.

Where there is a failure to respond appropriately, Jesus' second step entails taking along one or two others for a second meeting. The initial attempt to win the brother round is repeated, this time in the presence of witnesses. Should this fail, the third step is to bring the problem to the attention of the local church. If the offending party declines to respond to the discipline of the church, the ultimate sanction is exclusion from the fellowship, treating the offender like an outsider.

The intended outcome of the whole process of church discipline is not merely to bring a necessary rebuke, but far more importantly, to work for genuine repentance and personal reconciliation.

The whole tenor of such a conversation is never designed to be negative or to condemn. The underlying motivation should be nothing but supportive, encouraging and full of grace. Even the ultimate sanction of exclusion is designed to bring about reconciliation, both with God and with the church: the door is always left open, should the offending party be prepared to repent.

We see these principles in action in Paul's correspondence with the Corinthian church. At first he calls them to expel anyone who 'calls himself a brother but is sexually immoral or greedy, an idolater or a slanderer, a drunkard or a swindler'. He even tells them not to share a meal with such a person (1 Corinthians 5:11). However, once the offender has shown sorrowful repentance and has abandoned his immorality, Paul urges them to 'forgive and comfort him, so that he will not be overwhelmed by excessive sorrow'. He therefore urges them to reaffirm their love for the person he previously commanded them to exclude. What's more, if the church are now prepared to forgive and restore the repentant offender, Paul explicitly states that he will add his personal forgiveness to theirs (2 Corinthians 2:7–10). What we loose on earth in the name of Christ, is loosed in heaven (Matthew 18:18).

Jesus' teaching was concerned with how to tackle issues of personal sin and conflict within the local church. However, these principles of church discipline and conflict management can readily be applied on a wider scale. Disagreements, rumours and controversies may all be dealt with wisely by using the same procedure, checking out details face to face, working for reconciliation, bringing in witnesses at an early stage, and avoiding raising the stakes through going public prematurely. It should hardly surprise us that when Jesus' clear instructions are ignored, minor disputes escalate into major conflagrations. Those who fail to consult properly in private, are the terrorists of evangelical controversy. They have the power to cause an excessive and unwarranted explosion in public, causing irresponsible, disproportionate and unnecessary injuries among innocent Christian bystanders.

Truth and unity

In Acts 15 Luke records two significant disputes in the early church. In the first, there is a 'sharp dispute and debate' about the correct policy over circumcision among Gentile converts (Acts 15:2). The contenders are Paul and Barnabas, who argue that the rite is entirely superfluous for Gentile believers, and the Judaisers, whose ardent conviction is that the Jewish rite should be retained. The basis of the dispute is the doctrine of salvation, for the Judaisers insist that, without circumcision according to the custom taught by Moses, 'you cannot be saved' (Acts 15:1). Ultimately, as Paul was to demonstrate in his letter to the Galatians, such a debate is centred on the atonement. Either the cross of Christ fulfils the law and secures complete salvation, or additional rites remain necessary, an indispensable contribution to our standing before God. For the apostle, to circumcise Gentile Christians is not merely to impose an irrelevant custom, it undermines the power of the cross and therefore in limiting the effectiveness of his self-sacrifice demeans Christ himself. In imposing circumcision, the well-intentioned Judaisers robbed their Gentile converts of the full and free salvation that is assured through the cross of Christ alone.

This critical dispute could not be resolved in Antioch, and so it was referred to a higher authority, the apostles and elders in Jerusalem. Once the council began, the believers belonging to the party of the Pharisees were given the opportunity to speak first, and they defended their position with a clear and robust appeal to the law of Moses (Acts 15:5). As for the case against circumcision, there were four key contributors. Peter recounted the initial outpouring of the Holy Spirit upon Gentile believers, when Cornelius' household received the Spirit, just as the Jewish believers had at Pentecost (Acts 10–11;15:8–9). Paul and Barnabas then gave testimony, providing an eyewitness account of the miraculous signs and wonders that God had been pleased to perform among the Gentiles during their ministry (Acts 15:12). Finally, the apostle James presented the case from the Scriptures that the prophets had foretold a time when God would draw many Gentiles to living faith. Just as Peter concluded that the Spirit of God makes no distinction between Jewish and Gentile Christians, James roundly condemned any attempt to impose the Jewish ritual law: 'We should not make it difficult for the Gentiles who are turning to God' (Acts 15:13–21).

The decision of the Council of Jerusalem was definitive: circumcision was not to be imposed upon Gentile converts. In this dispute it was therefore recognised that the Judaising party was in the wrong, despite the fact that their argument was based on the law of Moses and they thought of themselves as Bible believing Christians. They were overcome by three key factors: the indisputable work of the Spirit, the unmistakable teaching of the Word, and the thorough deliberation and careful decision of the apostles. Because the first Christians recognised that genuine unity is dependent upon a common commitment to the truth of the gospel, their decision meant the effective exclusion from the church of any unrepentant members of the circumcision party. Unity before truth would have led to compromise and uncertainty. Unity built upon truth led to the need to disagree, and the public declaration of the official policy of the Church.

Secondary disputes and unity

The second disagreement in Acts 15 has an entirely different feel. The issue is the recruitment policy for an apostolic ministry team (Acts 15:36–41), and this time the contenders are Paul and Barnabas, previously allies in the circumcision dispute. The basis of this 'sharp disagreement' is judgement of character, namely their contrasting assessments of the suitability of John Mark, who had deserted their team not long before. Barnabas wants to give John Mark another chance without delay. Paul considers this kindness to be premature, fearing that the young man will only get in the way. It would, of course, be a mistake to imagine that Paul wrote off John Mark entirely, since he referred to him some years later as a helpful and dependable colleague (2 Timothy 4:11).

Behind the presenting issue of John Mark's reliability we can identify two contrasting temperaments that result in two different approaches to teamwork. Barnabas, who is more pastorally motivated, is concerned to build *a relational team*, in which the effectiveness of the team in the task of mission grows out of the quality of mutual support and relationship among the team members. Paul, who is more evangelistic, is concerned to build *a task-oriented team*, in which personal needs within the team are subordinated to the primary task of active evangelism. One begins with relationships, the other with the task. For Barnabas, the effective delivery of the evangelistic task will grow out of the development of strong relationships. For Paul, the relationships will grow out of the effective implementation of the task. There is no right and wrong about these two approaches. They simply reflect two different kinds of team, derived from contrasting temperaments and disparate styles of leadership. The problem here is not that one party is in error, but rather that the underlying assumptions and approaches of Paul and Barnabas to team building and team leadership are incompatible.

This second critical dispute involving Paul and Barnabas is not referred to the Jerusalem apostles for decision. It is not a matter of fundamental doctrine, but of divergent working practices. Both Paul and Barnabas were resolved not to turn disagreement between brothers into a slanging match. Their priority was not unity as an end in itself, which could have led to a paralysis of indecision, in which they were incapable of making any progress at all. Rather their priority was to get the task done. Their unity in mission was best expressed by their getting on with the job in separate teams, while flatly refusing to denounce one another's ministry on the basis of a serious disagreement about a secondary issue. Because they were able to retain unity in the faith, the indirect result of what must have seemed a traumatic and distressing difference of opinion was an unintentional increase in activity devoted to world mission. Where there had been a single church-planting team sent out from Antioch, there were now two teams hard at work. Their separation was therefore not disastrous. In the same way, the presence of more than one evangelical church in a town is not in itself a denial of unity in truth. Handled correctly, with mutual respect and appreciation, diversity in our styles of leadership and evangelistic programmes can positively enhance our unity in mission. Paul and Barnabas did not need to waste time in an abortive attempt to browbeat one another into uniformity. Their example demonstrates that we can do things differently and separately from one another, without compromising our essential unity in truth and in mission.

The limits of unity

The Jerusalem Council and the New Testament practice of church discipline both indicate the limits of evangelical unity. Where there is fundamental heresy or undeniable immorality, unity is no longer the first priority, or even an option. In the modern church, just as in the first century, *unity in truth* will inevitably lead to disagreements and exclusions, just as the Judaisers were excluded by the Jerusalem Council. The danger is that warm-hearted evangelicals may be reluctant ever to draw a line in the sand and speak out against fundamental error. However, in accepting the limits of unity, it is essential that we do not raise the stakes too high over those secondary issues where evangelicals disagree among themselves. We should never betray our unity in the essentials of orthodoxy for the sake of some relatively trivial dispute. Unity in truth sets a limit on unity, faced with those who do not embrace the essential gospel, however much we may agree on secondary issues. Unity in truth also sets a limit on disunity for all who hold fast to the gospel, whatever our differences over secondary issues.

At the same time, *unity in mission* will prompt us to commend the evangelistic initiatives of other evangelicals, whether or not we are taking part, or would even consider taking part, in their particular programme. Once the Jerusalem Council had made its decision, Paul considered himself to be at perfect liberty to denounce the circumcision party as 'mutilators of the flesh' (Philippians 3:2). However, we do not have a record of a single harsh word spoken by Paul or Barnabas against the other's missionary methods or team. Their disagreement was never a basis for continued public dispute or divisiveness.

This second dimension of apostolic unity and disagreement serves to remind us that we are working in a common cause, without necessarily always working in a single team. In evangelistic purpose we need to remain united, even when in our evangelistic activities different tribes of evangelicals will employ divergent styles and approaches. Working together, these two levels of unity, in truth and in mission, will lead to an absolute refusal to unchurch those who share our core convictions, even though in secondary matters they may be altogether different to us. The apostolic commission has not changed: we have a gospel to guard and a world to win, and we can only accomplish these things effectively if we maintain the two strands of our unity, in truth and in mission.

Holy disagreement

May they be brought to complete unity
to let the world know that you sent me (John 17:23).
Make every effort to keep the unity of the Spirit
through the bond of peace. (Ephesians 4:3).

Since the New Testament places such a high priority upon unity, we need to ensure that every effort really is made to maintain unity. An historical example of just such an initiative is found in the practical resolutions of the General Assembly that inaugurated the Evangelical Alliance in the United Kingdom in 1846. They have been included in this book in appendix 2.

The only kind of disagreement we can allow ourselves to be part of must be a *holy disagreement*, whether in uncompromising but courteous defence of the truth, or in agreeing to differ with fellow Christians, with whom we nonetheless remain united in truth and in our common mission, Our wider unity needs to be declared, so that our words and attitudes affirm our common cause in the truth of the gospel. Our unity also needs to be demonstrated wherever possible by sharing public platforms, and by refusing to become part of an isolated and exclusive enclave, with a sectarian mind set.

When we oppose other believers, for whatever reason, we need to speak in grace, with gentleness, kindness and love. We need to affirm them as Christians and express appreciation for their gifts and the dedication of their ministry. When we have no choice but to disagree, we need to adhere to the clear procedures laid down by Jesus, to avoid needless and premature escalation of a controversy. We should always devote more words to private prayer on behalf of our opponents than to public criticism.

There is nothing more regrettable than an evangelical whose convictions you share, behaving during a controversy in a manner that is deeply disagreeable. Both our attitudes and our words need to be measured for true integrity and holiness. There is no room for any resentment, hostility or bitterness of heart in a holy disagreement, nor for any measure of intemperate denunciation or exaggeration. It is all too easy to impugn the motives or actions of another Christian, and all too difficult to undo the damage, once such poison has been injected into a dispute. For myself, I have to confess there have been times when I have needed to repent of my attitude towards those I still believe it was right and necessary to oppose.

Above all, where there needs to be disagreement among evangelicals, essential matters must be given priority. In the heat of controversy we easily end up majoring on minors, making a mountainous dispute out of a relatively trivial difference. Where there needs to be disagreement, we need to begin by affirming all that we hold in common. If we are to ensure that we preserve true unity and engage only in holy disagreement, these traditional evangelical values must remain a touchstone for us in every dispute:

> In essentials, immovable;
> In non-essentials, flexible;
> And in all things, grace and truth.

10

The futures of evangelicalism

Evangelicals are on the march. Our numbers are growing, and we are steadily attracting more attention from the media. After decades in which evangelicals were a marginalised remnant, holding faithfully to the gospel in the context of a society and theological consensus that were indifferent and even hostile to evangelical convictions, we breathe the heady air of relative success. But there is no room for triumphalism. As we consider our prospects in the new millennium, we need to recognise that there are several futures for evangelicalism. If we are serious about building for the future, then all need to be faced as genuine possibilities, even though some are distinctly unpalatable.

Retaining the status quo

Although more of the same is hardly the most exciting prospect, it certainly remains a distinct possibility. A great deal of effort has been put into establishing the present measure of mutual respect and understanding among evangelicals. At first sight this might indicate that the present patterns of co-operation are fairly secure. Nonetheless, the fault lines within evangelicalism and also within the historic denominations suggest that the continuance of the status quo is an increasingly unlikely prospect.

Reassimilation

When the Anglo-Catholic movement in the Church of England was at its peak of influence, many suggested that a change in the essential character of Anglicanism was almost inevitable. However, when a number of senior Anglo-Catholics were appointed as bishops, almost at once they began to speak in terms of serving the whole of a broad church. At the same time, other leading lights in the movement began to play down their Anglo-Catholic characteristics with one eye on the possibility of future preferment for those who were seen not to rock the boat. While they never entirely abandoned them, their distinctive emphases became diluted. They no longer held out the serious possibility of a re-catholicisation of the Church of England in their generation. Gradually the Anglo-Catholics were assimilated into the Anglican mainstream, no more a movement for fundamental reforms that were threatening or contentious to other Anglicans, but rather one further distinctive tradition within the Anglican communion.

This historical precedent serves as a clear warning to evangelicals, who have now attained in several denominations a position of numerical strength and recognition not seen for many decades. The number of bishops, superintendents and other senior leaders coming from the evangelical stable has steadily increased in recent years. But will the trans-denominational distinctivenesses of our evangelical convictions survive such advancement? Or will senior evangelicals become increasingly distanced from one another as their energies are poured into their denominational duties? The evangelical advance could yet be dispelled by an increasingly denominational focus, particularly among senior leaders, with a corresponding diminution of evangelical identity and concern.

Reform

While evangelicals could lose themselves in a process of reassimilation that would long remain imperceptible, the opposite prospect also remains a distinct possibility. That is, following numerical growth in evangelical churches and the increasing prominence of evangelical leaders within the denominations, the evangelicals could bring about substantial denominational reform. In doctrine and ethics, there has been a steady drift in several denominations towards a liberal theological consensus and towards a compromise with the moral standards of the late twentieth century. In their priorities, many denominations and local churches have been committed more to maintenance than mission: looking after the saints in familiar and comfortable ways rather than reaching the unbelievers. Should the present numerical advance continue unabated, and should the prominent and influential leaders not falter in their grip upon evangelical basics, a remarkable and perhaps unprecedented development could come about during the next decade: a genuine and thoroughgoing evangelical reform of existing and historic denominations.

The witness of history tells us that evangelical reform movements have almost invariably found it easier to start a new denomination than to turn around one already in existence. What's more, we are already seeing more hardline evangelical reformers, notably in the Anglican church, begin to turn their guns upon their fellow evangelicals. One leader's slow and patient work for reform is another leader's sell-out to the status quo. In short, even within the historic denominations, some evangelicals' instinctive approach is separatist rather than believing in the slow process of reform from within.

The inertia of religious institutions should not be underestimated. There is seductive, resilient and powerful cultural bias in favour of the status quo to be found within the committee structures and customary procedures of any organisation more than a hundred years old. The reluctance of Christians to cause more disarray or disruption than is absolutely necessary means that some who have entered the denominational structures as reformers have later confessed to losing their way, not knowing how to move forward an institution so capable of ensuring its self-perpetuation. Evangelical reform of the historic denominations seems a genuine prospect, but it can hardly be said to be assured as yet.

Refragmentation

An embattled, frequently patronised and sometimes even persecuted evangelical minority has learned to rally together in defence of the cause. The danger of sustained growth is that evangelicals could become more casual or even hotheaded about the possible consequences of disagreeing with one another. The luxury of greater numbers is that we no longer feel isolated and alone if we isolate ourselves from other evangelicals within our own exclusive and increasingly sectarian tribe.

We identified in chapter 5 an immense stockpile of disagreements that could easily explode at any time. The greatest irony of evangelical growth in the past quarter century could be that the indirect consequence of such growth is that evangelicals become complacent about self-destructive tendencies. We could become content to dispute with one another with increasing animosity and venom, rather than commit ourselves in unity to the fundamental priorities we hold in common: guarding the gospel and winning the world. Refragmentation is a real but disastrous prospect, should evangelicals choose the easy and yet palpably absurd option of devoting their energies to warring with one another.

Remnant

We suggested in chapter 6 that there is evidence to suggest a corrosion in evangelical convictions. Some are engaged in a theological journey towards a kind of semi-orthodoxy, from where they survey more traditional evangelicals with a dismissive, even patronising superiority. There is no one more resistant to evangelicals than an ex-evangelical. Others are muting, or even moving away from their previous evangelical convictions for reasons of ecclesiastical or academic career. Still others have become biblically semi-literate, and therefore less discriminating about the teaching they find acceptable. Whatever the origins or motivation of such corrosion it leads to the same question: when does an evangelical cease to be an evangelical?

The bleakest prospect is not that evangelicals go to war with

one another, but rather that some evangelicals come to disown
their inheritance, entering a post-evangelical, mild-mannered and
moderate liberalism. Should such a trend become dominant, all
that would be left after the decades of evangelical resurgence
would be, once again, a remnant of the faithful and orthodox.

Realignment

The witness of history gives cause to doubt whether the structural
realignment of Christianity is a realistic possibility. Whatever the
levels of frustration or disillusion ministers may suffer towards
their denomination, the self-interest of a career structure and a
pension scheme brings a great deal of inertia. What is more, there
is always the fear that the initial separatists may end up marginalised and isolated, should others decline to join them, such as
happened to Spurgeon when he left the Baptist Union. The spectre
of Martyn Lloyd-Jones' invitation to those in mixed denominations and John Stott's equally strong repudiation of separatism,
still casts shadows over such a prospect for evangelicals. Lloyd-
Jones' call to a new evangelical unity backfired dramatically,
resulting in severe disunity and the reassertion of the priority of
distinctive denominational identities. Nonetheless, we can identify
a number of critical factors that point towards the possibility of a
general realignment of Christians. Should this begin to occur,
evangelicals may have new choices to make, as some groupings
become more remote, or even openly resistant to evangelical
convictions, while others become more distinctly and overtly
evangelical in doctrine and practice.

We are yet to see how far evangelicals in historic denominations
can influence their denominations' future trajectories. A quarter
of a century of dedicated denominational participation has led to
an evangelical prominence across the board. Will the evangelicals
change the status quo, or will the status quo change the evangelicals? Should there be little evidence of real progress, the rising
generation of evangelicals may become disillusioned with the
priority of denominational loyalty, and look primarily once again
to a trans-denominational, or possibly even a post-denominational
evangelical unity.

The current process in Christian ethics of accelerating compromise with the moral standards of the day, may yet provoke some evangelicals to depart from their denominations. Some will almost certainly conclude that the bridge too far will be the acceptance of living together and settled homosexual relationships as legitimate and authentic equivalents to monogamous, heterosexual marriage. If such evangelicals conclude that they have no choice but to secede, they will need to find an appropriate new home, where evangelical doctrine and ethics are secure and guaranteed.

A further dimension to realignment could be found among those Christians who practise believers' baptism. Long a tiny minority of Christians in Western Europe, the number of baptistic Christians is accelerating rapidly across the world. The fastest growing denominations and streams in many countries are the Pentecostals, followed by the independents and the new churches. Among the historic denominations, the Baptists have suffered less inroads from liberalism and consequently less numerical decline. In Britain, while the Anglican church is far larger than the Baptists, these two groups have roughly the same representation at evangelical gatherings as the two largest evangelical tribes.

For Baptists and Anabaptists, their history has been characterised by their baptismal convictions causing an unavoidable and irretractable detachment from other Christians. During the Reformation, both Catholics and the magisterial reformers were united in one resolve: the persecution and even execution of those who practised believers' baptism. The West is now catching up with the rest of the world: believers' baptism is becoming the conviction and practice of an increasing proportion of evangelicals. It remains to be seen whether Baptists, Pentecostals and new churches will remain separate from one another or will be able to pursue new kinds of co-operation and coalition.

Traditionalist Baptists have consistently put much more effort into respectable and establishment ecumenism with the historic denominations. What's more, British Baptists have historically been more strongly committed to congregational government than Baptists in other parts of the world, many of whom practise various kinds of presbyterianism. The curious result has been British Baptists frequently at odds with fellow believer-baptising churches over patterns of church government, while courting those 'respectable' historic denominations who practise neither congregational government nor believers' baptism. The self-evident truth remains that Baptists' closest cousins are in fact the Pentecostals and the new churches. Is it too farfetched to suggest that believer-baptising evangelicals might find new ways of networking, in which diverse streams in terms of ethos and church government would relate together much more closely than at present? Such a coalition would derive unity from the bedrock of shared evangelical convictions, the priority of evangelism and the initiatory practice of believers' baptism.

It seems open to question whether Anglicanism can survive as a single church, faced with three powerful and fragmentary trends that it will be difficult to reverse: the increasing number of departures to Rome, particularly following the ordination of women; the growth of an evangelical reform movement, that, while it does not represent all evangelicals, seems increasingly separatist, congregational, and resistant to the conventional patterns of compromise in the Anglican *via media*; and thirdly a cultural momentum that begins to make eventual disestablishment look inevitable, perhaps within the next twenty years. If the Anglican consensus did indeed come unstuck, in addition to the crises and opportunities provoked by the factors we have just explored, the likelihood would increase enormously of a wider and substantial realignment of the Christian churches.

Should such a realignment begin to happen, it might take on something like the following pattern. We could see a resurgent Catholicism, embracing not only Anglo-Catholics, but a wider grouping of orthodox Christians who accept a Catholic and episcopal framework to the organisation and leadership of the church. We could also be faced with a disestablished Church of England, Protestant and Reformed, mainly for those who are broadly evangelical in conviction and liturgical in worship. Such a grouping would mainly comprise evangelical Anglicans. A Liberal Free Church would increasingly assimilate those in the present free churches who accept a liberal framework of doctrine and ethics, together with a traditional free church style of worship. This group would be the natural home for that tiny minority of Baptists who are liberal and Free Church, for whom believers' baptism represents a negotiable custom rather than an immovable conviction. If evangelicals reach the point of concluding that they have no choice in all integrity but to depart from one or more of the present historic Free Churches, some would gravitate more naturally to an evangelical Anglican setting, while others would more readily identify with the baptistic churches. These churches represent the fourth sector in such a realignment of the church, and on present statistics, they would probably represent the majority of evangelicals, and are certainly at present the sector enjoying the most rapid numerical growth. They would come together in a coalition or network of streams of those who are evangelical, non-liturgical, and believer-baptising. This fourth grouping would also be predominantly, and also increasingly should present trends continue, Pentecostal or charismatic. These then are the four main sectors of a denominational realignment: Catholics (and Orthodox); Low Church evangelical Anglicans; liberal and traditional free churches; evangelical and believer-baptising free churches. What of the middle-of-the-road, liberal Anglicans? On present trends, with elderly and shrinking congregations, they are well on the way to extinction. We have stated that the prospects for such a realignment are doubtful, but the possibilities remain intriguing. While some will meet the very suggestion of such a prospect with derision or horror, others will doubtless find such a future attractive, or even a source of hope and expectancy.

Renewal

After thirty years of charismatic renewal, no denomination has been left untouched. On present trends, by the end of the century no less than one half of all evangelicals will identify themselves as charismatics. The revolution in worship has been largely stimulated by charismatics, and the wider church is increasingly open to the possibility of healing ministry and the exercise of spiritual gifts.

For all the impact of renewal, the movement itself has reached a crossroads. As the survivors from among the early leaders draw near to retirement, leadership needs to be passed to a new generation. This is a critical moment in the life cycle of any

Christian organisation or grouping, when an outward looking movement can turn in upon itself, becoming a monument, an institution with a great past and a small future. Many Christian groupings have been unable to make the transition from reliance upon the key founder to dependence upon a succession of leaders. There is a danger of losing much momentum without the exceptional vision and creative drive that the original leaders brought to the cause. Leadership development is therefore a crucial priority for older leaders, who need increasingly to be less concerned about providing the ministry themselves, and more concerned about providing support and opportunities for those who are emerging as their successors.

The second critical factor at this crossroads for renewal is the need to demonstrate in practice the integration of Word and Spirit. The dynamic commitment to these twin priorities was fundamental to the ministry of the Apostle Paul. He reminded the Thessalonians that he not only preached the Word of Truth, but it was followed and authenticated by demonstrations of divine power (1 Thessalonians 1:5). In the same way, he reminded the Corinthians of their foundational commitment to the truth of the gospel – 'when you are assembled in the name of Jesus' – but at the same time he expected the Spirit of God to be unmistakably manifest in their meetings – 'and the power of the Lord Jesus is present'(1 Corinthians 5:4).

In reaction against dry orthodoxy, which was dedicated to the Word but indifferent, suspicious, or even hostile to the Spirit, charismatics have sometimes appeared to overthrow the Word in favour of the Spirit. If renewal is to advance into genuine and lasting maturity, the double commitments to Word and Spirit must be its foundation. Where we embrace both Word and Spirit, we repudiate the old and false dichotomies and become concerned about both the mind and the heart, our understanding of doctrine and the experiences of our walk with God. If there is a thoughtful and pervasive acceptance of this apostolic combination of submission to revealed truth and yielding to the Spirit's power, we can reasonably expect in the coming decades further advances in mission, growth and renewal.

Revival

The greatest prospect is the one most beyond our control. While we can pray for revival, it cannot be manufactured. Historically, two of the most significant indicators that a revival may soon follow have been a growing sense of despair in society at the consequences of godless living, together with a profound sense of weakness in the church. Revival seems invariably to be preceded by an acute sense of need among many believers. That does not mean that a sense of need guarantees that revival will automatically follow, but the opposite does seem to be inevitable: where there is complacency, no revival will come. The impact of the eighteenth-century revival was well summed up by J. R. Green.

> A religious revival burst forth ... which changed in a few years the whole temper of English society. The Church was restored to life and activity. Religion carried to the hearts of the people a fresh spirit of moral zeal, while it purified our literature and our manners. A new philanthropy reformed our prisons, infused clemency and wisdom into our penal laws, abolished the slave trade, and gave the first impulse to popular education.[1]

While recognising all the dangers of an exaggerated sense of the place of Britain in the modern world, we nonetheless suggest that should revival break out in these years, British evangelicals have a potentially pivotal contribution to make. The English language is the most effective means of communicating a revival around the world. Across the countries of the commonwealth, Christians still look with favour upon Christian initiatives from Britain, for British Christians were often the first to bring Christianity to their land. We not only have good access to North America, thanks to our common language, but we also have close cultural connections with the rest of Europe. Indeed, when I was a publisher, my European colleagues frequently told me that British teaching books generally worked better than American books in their countries, simply because the cultural differences are much smaller. By culture and temperament, the British are not inclined to extremism, sensationalism or emotionalism, so that, if some of the unusual phenomena typically linked to periods of revival are seen in Britain, other nations may sit up and take notice. We have also been extremely fortunate in avoiding the false antithesis prevalent in many parts of the world, where believers often consider themselves to be either evangelicals or charismatics, in two separate and mutually exclusive camps. Because charismatic and non-charismatic evangelicals have been seeking to co-operate as much as possible in Britain for many years, we are well placed not only to take the initiative in demonstrating an effective integration of Word and Spirit, but also to provide a framework of reflection and direction for any movements that are pressing towards revival.

While we cannot guarantee revival, it should never be discounted. In actual fact an increasing number of evangelical leaders believe revival to be a real prospect for the Western world in this generation, and I readily include myself among them. When Isaac Watts heard of the Great Awakening in America, his first thought was to stir up British Christians to pray for a similar outpouring of the mighty and merciful power of the living God. Once again in this generation we look for a yearning for revival to find passionate expression in the fervent prayers of all evangelical Christians.

As we face these various futures, we need to be clear in our evangelical convictions, committed to unity in the face of secondary disagreements, and prayerful for the advance of the gospel that has been guarded so faithfully by evangelicals in generation after generation. One thing is certain about the future of evangelicalism: if revival comes, our worst fears will be overthrown and our best hopes will pale into insignificance.

> *Now to him who is able to do immeasurably more than all we ask or imagine, according to his power that is at work within us, to him be glory in the church and in Christ Jesus throughout all generations, for ever and ever! Amen (Ephesians 3:20–1).*

Appendix 1

An evangelical consultation on 'The Toronto Blessing'

In relation to what has come to be known as 'the Toronto Blessing', a consultation of some leading evangelicals recognised the need not only to evaluate such experiences but also to make clear distinctions between primary and secondary convictions among us. We therefore reaffirm the overwhelming measure of agreement among us as evangelicals, even though we differ in our initial interpretations of these experiences.

1) We affirm together the classic evangelical convictions. The Scriptures are the inspired Word of God; our faith is centred on the person and atoning work of Christ; we stress the vital need for personal conversion; we are committed to active witness and service in the world.

2) We affirm the centrality of the Great Commission to the task of the church. We also rejoice that in our history God has poured out his Spirit in revivals, and these are intrinsic to the evangelical heritage we share.

3) We affirm the indivisible unity of the Word and Spirit. The Scriptures are God-breathed and their authority cannot be diminished. The Holy Spirit who inspired the unchanging Scriptures applies them to our lives, to both our minds and our hearts. We seek to live under the authority of the Word and in the power of

the Spirit. The essence of work of the Spirit according to the Scriptures includes the following:

> Christ is central and glorified.
> Hunger grows for the Word and for prayer.
> Awareness of the holiness of God leads to repentance and holiness of life.
> Spiritual gifts are distributed and exercised in the church.
> Preaching becomes empowered.
> The love and joy of God are poured into our hearts.
> Greater passion arises for the lost, without God and without hope.
> Greater compassion arises for the disadvantaged, demonstrated in social action.

Where the Spirit's work is intensified, we would expect to see a heightened awareness of these distinctives.

4) The Spirit of God comes to clothe the church with power from on high, both in the ongoing process of continuing church life and growth, and also in dramatic periods of revival.

5) Where we differ, we remain committed to evangelical unity, based on our common convictions and priorities under the Lordship of Christ. We confess that in the past this unity has sometimes been undermined by a failure to listen to one another, and by a readiness to caricature and denigrate those with whom we disagree. In this consultation we have sought to ask questions of ourselves and one another, without compromising the integrity of our conscientiously held differences.

6) Where there have been revivals, there has generally been an increase in the frequency of manifestations associated with repentance and conversion and also with the joy of new and abundant life in Christ. However, we are all clear that these manifestations are secondary. Physical and emotional manifestations cannot in themselves prove that a movement is or is not a work of God. The test is the lasting, biblical fruit. No one should seek manifestations

as an end in themselves. Rather, we need to seek to grow in the knowledge of God and in his service.

7) At present we are inevitably seeing that experience is not yet integrated with theological reflection. We rejoice with those who have known genuine life-changing encounters with the holiness and majesty, power and love of the risen Christ. We reject any tendency to pursue manifestations as an end in themselves. We regret that some have neglected the discipline of biblical preaching in the face of current manifestations, but we rejoice with those who speak of a new empowering in preaching in recent months. Our common priority is the proclamation of the gospel on fire.

8) We recognise that historical, theological and cultural influences can unconsciously condition our Christian perspective. The existentialist spirit of our age emphasises subjective experiences and feelings over convictions and objective truth. We also recognise the equal and opposite danger of enlightenment rationalism, which has in the past resulted in dead orthodoxy which leaves no room for the direct intervention of the Spirit of God. We must guard and proclaim the absolute truth of the gospel without compromise.

9) We do not believe that the church in the United Kingdom is presently experiencing revival. However, many have testified to an increased sense of the manifest presence of God in recent months, and to empowered preaching and conversions. This enrichment has been observed in some measure across the evangelical spectrum. This encourages us to hope that we may be in a period of preparation for revival.

10) The evaluation of present phenomena can only be provisional: it is too early for definitive judgements. While no work of God takes place without a fleshly dimension, or even the possibility of demonic counterfeit, opinions differ markedly among evangelicals at present over precisely what is happening. Some have grave reservations about the value and significance of recent events in many churches; others speak of 1994 as a year of remarkable spiritual refreshing. We therefore recognise the need for a group within the Evangelical Alliance to continue to provide evaluation

and theological reflection on these developments in the church. We suggest that such a group should plan to review these questions in a year's time.

11) We readily endorse the classic tests of a genuine work of God, as expounded by Jonathan Edwards:

> Does it raise people's estimation of Jesus Christ?
> Does it operate against the interests of Satan?
> Does it lead to a greater regard for Scripture and truth?
> Does it result in a greater awareness of and seriousness about the things of God?
> Does it lead to a greater love for God, for other Christians and for the wider world?

12) Our nations, and indeed our continent and world, are in desperate need of the Gospel. We therefore commit ourselves afresh to obey the command to proclaim the Good News and make disciples, and call the church to pray for the outpouring of the Spirit of God in revival power upon our land.

Appendix 2

The 1846 practical resolutions of the Evangelical Alliance

As fellow members of the Evangelical Alliance:

1. We encourage one another in making public comment to place the most charitable construction on the statements made by fellow Christians and particularly those who are members of the Alliance and, where expressions of disagreement are made, to do so with courtesy, humility and graciousness. (Ephesians 4:31)

2. We seek to bring the purposes of the Alliance to God in regular prayer and especially during the annual week of prayer.

3. We call on each other, where issues of faith and practice divide us, to take care that when we offer correction that this is done with awareness of our own failings (whether as individuals or churches) and the possibility that we ourselves may be mistaken. (Ephesians 4:15)

4. We urge each other, at all times when matters of theology are in dispute, to avoid personal hostility and abuse, speaking the truth in love and gentleness. (Ephesians 4:15)

5. We recognise that not all who seek to know and serve Christ as Saviour and Lord will wish to be members of the Alliance and that such persons are not, thereby, to be regarded as being out of Christian fellowship.

6. We urge all Christian leaders of Trinitarian churches to promote peace, unity and fellowship within the Body of Christ.

7. We wish to encourage all Christians to commit themselves to biblical truth and to that end, we pray that everyone including those of other or no religions may find in Christ true hope and salvation.

8. We rejoice in the spread of the Christian gospel across the world and thank God for its advance, also acknowledging the tensions which this has sometimes brought, and longing for the completion of Christ's Kingdom of peace and justice, to the glory of the one God, Father, Son and Holy Spirit.

> Make every effort to keep the unity of the Spirit
> through the bond of peace (Ephesians 4:3).

Afterword: Evangelical Unity

All of us have those moments when someone brings to our attention an obvious piece of information which we had managed to overlook. Such was my experience when a good friend pointed me to a passage from Isaiah 41:19,20 during a lunch meeting. I am definitely not a tree specialist, but the startling truth of the text became immediately apparent. The list of trees – the acacia, cedar, myrtle and olive, etc. – were totally incompatible in the same soil but God himself would plant them together for his own glory. The similarity would therefore be in the soil and the planter rather than the individual characteristics of each of the trees.

It is probably one of the best biblical illustrations for the theme of unity in diversity which has become so important for those of us working in multi-denominational or cross-cultural ministries. It is certainly noteworthy for any discussion on evangelical unity.

Any discussion on evangelical unity in the current climate is an adventurous undertaking. But it is also an unavoidable debate for evangelicals given the growing international profile of evangelical-ism as it sweeps across the church landscape in what a Latin American church leader described as a 'holy contagion'! But the exercise is thwarted with difficulties, not least because of the cultural and theological nuances involved in an international movement, but also because evangelicals are beginning to wonder if they all mean the same things by using the labels 'evangelical' and 'unity'.

Evangelical redefined

The current question is: 'What is an evangelical anyway?' or as David Coffey, General Secretary of the Baptist Union, put it: 'When is an evangelical **not** an evangelical?'

Certainly, within the United Kingdom 'evangelical' has increasingly become regarded as a noun, which means that it has acquired a measure of flexibility allowing it to embrace historic churches, pentecostals and new churches alike. Unlike the United States or Europe, for example, evangelical is a more inclusive label and is less likely to be used as a synonym for a non-pentecostal/charismatic position.

Our discussion about evangelical identity is therefore an important one and what we do with the label is not a matter of casual pursuits. Striving for acceptable biblical parameters by which to determine and define a biblical community is at the heart of the New Testament. Inevitably it will also touch on what we understand by **the church** and **the truth**. The label will always have its limitations and there will always be sincere, Bible-believing Christians who sit uncomfortably with it, but at least it tends to force the issues and keeps these important items on the agenda.

The great challenge to modern evangelicalism, I suggest, will be the need to maintain its links with its biblical and historic heritage while developing a cutting edge adequate for the millennium and distinguishable in the twilight zone of modern relativism.

Unity in diversity

It goes without saying that no one wants **uniformity**. It is not desirable, biblical or achievable. Evangelicals have a notional agreement that we are all called to conform only so far as we are conformed to the image of Christ. This takes us back to the common-soil analogy we started with and gives us the basis for our unity. If we are truly together, we are together **in Him**.

Real unity goes beyond evangelical labels. It is more profound than what evangelicals do together. Evangelical unity is therefore beyond an evangelical's ability to produce and is mediated by the

Holy Spirit from the heart of God. So unity is **given** not gained. In a sense, we cannot help being united but to some measure we may be able to help ourselves from being divided. And there is quite a lot which threatens our growing and as yet fragile unity.

Crossing the evangelical streams

My own feeling is that denominationalism is the least of our problems. Label-loyalty has lost its grip over us as a result of social mobility and the shrinking evangelical world. The denominational melt-down has come about for a number of inter-related reasons but there is little doubt that a new international mind set has been stimulated by popular media and the new networking culture promoted by our numerous conferences, consultations and joint celebrations. Two things have recently exemplified this for me. One was observing the warm and long-standing partnership between the Vineyard leader, John Wimber, and the Anglican bishop, David Pytches, during a New Wine Conference. The second was the recognition that Keswick Convention, which now has at least one Pentecostal on its Council, also includes songs from New Church authors in its programme song supplements. If you need a third example the growing relationship between Elim and Assemblies of God, culminating in their joint conference, is worth noting. With this degree of spiritual migration taking place, an ex-Brethren once New Church, now Anglican, is no longer an unlikely specimen of evangelical Christianity.

There has been a powerful cross-streaming in all kinds of activities and settings which has enriched evangelical unity and equally brought its own challenges in recent years. This has certainly been the case within the March for Jesus, Spring Harvest and Greenbelt events. The same is also true of the steady growth of the Proclamation Trust's expository ministry which has seen an influx of students from pentecostal backgrounds in recent years. In 1995 some 8,000 of the 21,500 guests at New Frontiers International were from other groups. This degree of interfacing is not necessarily reflected throughout evangelicalism in the UK. Significant movements such as the Crieff Brotherhood in Scotland, the Evangelical Movement of Wales, the Federation of Independent Churches and to a much lesser extent the British Evangelical Council would not reflect the same degree of pan-evangelicalism although many respected church leaders from within these ministries are well known and received beyond their own immediate frontiers.

Evangelical unity is also being worked out against a global setting. International ministries are talking together and attempting to complement each other. The distinctives between movements such as Lausanne and World Evangelical Fellowship (WEF) and AD 2000 remain evident but there is also a clear recognition of their evangelical status within their distinctive emphases. As the spotlight roams throughout the international evangelical community new moves for reconciliation among evangelicals give us some grounds for optimism as we have observed the renewed impetus of the European Evangelical movement, the emergence of an authentic South African Evangelical Alliance rising from the ashes of apartheid and the tentative steps of the National Association of Evangelicals to include and enfranchise Black and Hispanic Americans in a significant reshuffle during the last eighteen months. In 1994 the Pentecostal Association of North America became the Pentecostal and Charismatic Fellowship of North America.

Evangelical unity in evangelical diversity is proving to be no mere sentiment. We are also coming to see that unity is not another word for look-alike. That has undoubtedly been the ongoing lesson of British evangelicalism in recent years. In fact, Myles Monroe is very keen to remind us that diversity is *necessary* for unity. As he put it, 'You can only unite people who are different.'

Rocks Ahead

We want to be grateful for all recent happenings but we are equally aware that evangelical unity has a long way to go. Evangelicals in most countries are still minority groups and we still have some potential boulders in the way as the streams attempt to mingle in the flow of church life.

Within the historic churches women's ordination, attitudes

towards homosexuality and the feasibility of 'mixed congregations' will continue to present serious challenges for evangelicals within those churches and for friendships outside. Other issues such as ecumenism, eternal punishment, experience, phenomena and interpretation of Scripture are unlikely to go away quietly. As we approach the millennium the eschatological debate will no doubt resurface to demand more attention.

In all of this, I suspect that one of the greatest tests for evangelicals will be what our American friends call 'attitude'. The writing is already on the wall and it is becoming apparent that many evangelicals are strong on truth but weak on grace. Why can't we have both in equal dosages? I'm certain that this is the biblical prescription for error or misdemeanour. As we get our house in order, a watching world is more likely to exegete our graciousness than our propositions. The future of our authentic unity is likely to rely on the painful realisation that truth is always far more secure than theologies and that we can move our feet without losing ground. My own pilgrimage has shown me that truth has always been so much more generous and bigger than I had been led to believe.

Evangelical unity is therefore an important discussion about our collective identity as diverse Bible-believing individuals and communities. In our post-modern relativism the search after 'true truth', as Francis Schaeffer put it, is an imperative task – however hard the exercise. Christian activists who have little patience for definition need to beware they do not swap clarity about what a Christian is for Christian pragmatism.

This Christian unity cannot be merely structural or activity-driven. It is an essential unity of the Spirit which is maintained in the bonds of peace. But even more than that, it is a unity with a specific missological aim. Jesus' prayer made this very plain: 'May they be brought to complete unity to let the world know . . .' (John 17:23). We would do well to remember, then, that any notion of evangelical unity must be about a truth-based unity inculcated by the Holy Spirit with a view to bringing testimony to the Lordship of Christ. However difficult a subject, it is certainly worth writing and talking about.

JOEL EDWARDS

Notes

Chapter 1   See how these Christians love one another

1. Robert McAfee Brown, *The Spirit of Protestantism* New York, Oxford 1961.
2. See further, Clive Calver and Peter Meadows, *Dancing in the Dark* Oxford, Lynx 1994.
3. ed. Colin Brown, *New International Dictionary of New Testament Theology* Carlisle, Paternoster Press 1976.
4. ed. David Barrett, *The World Christian Encyclopedia* Oxford, OUP 1982.
5. John P. Baker, 'The Local Church in the Purpose of God' ed. J. P. Baker, *Christ's Living Body* London, Coverdale House 1973.
6. Rex A. Koivisto, *One Lord, One Faith* Wheaton, Ill., Victor Books 1993.
7. John P. Baker, 'Introduction' in ed. J. P. Baker.

Chapter 2   One in the Spirit

1. E. Jay, ed., *The Journal of John Wesley* Oxford 1988.
2. John Stott, *Christ The Controversialist* London, Tyndale Press, 1970.
3. Quoted in Derek Tidball, *Who Are The Evangelicals?* London, Marshall Pickering 1994.
4. Stott, *Christ the Controversialist*.
5. Clive Calver, Ian Coffey and Peter Meadows, *Who Do Evan-*

gelicals Think They Are? London, Evangelical Alliance 1993.
See also John Stott and David Edwards, *Essentials: A liberal-
evangelical dialogue* (London, Hodder & Stoughton 1988, and
Graham Kuhrt in ed. Alan Gibson, *The Church and Its Unity*
Leicester, IVP 1992.

6. Richard Holloway, 'Evangelicalism: An Outsider's Perspec-
tive' in R. T. France and A. E. McGrath (eds), *Evangelical
Anglicans: Their Role and Influence in the Church Today*
London, SPCK 1993.

7. R. T. France and A. E. McGrath p. 3.

8. Alistair McGrath, *Evangelicalism and the Future of Christianity* London, Hodder & Stoughton 1993.

9. John Stott, *What Is an Evangelical?* London, CPAS 1977.

10. John Stott in ed. John Allan, *The Evangelicals: An Illustrated
History* Exeter, WEF 1989.

11. Kenneth Myers, 'A Better Way: Proclamation Instead of
Protest' in ed. M. S. Horton, *Power Religion: The Selling Out
of the Evangelical Church* Chicago, Moody Press 1992.

12. Derek Tidball, p. 12.

Chapter 3 'Blest be the tie that binds'

1. Graham Kendrick, from the jacket of *'Paid on the Nail'*
Kingsway, Eastbourne 1973.

2. Michael Green and R. Paul Stevens, *New Testament Spirituality* Guildford, Eagle 1994.

3. John Fawcett, *Baptist Church Hymnal* London, The Baptist
Union Publication Dept 1933

4. J. Y. Campbell in *Journal of Biblical Literature* Vol. 51, 1932.
Ralph P. Martin, 'Communion' in *The Illustrated Bible
Dictionary* Leicester, IVP 1980.

5. Mark Birchall, 'Oh Blest Communion, fellowship divine'
unpublished, 1993.

6. Francis Schaeffer, 'Form and Freedom in the Church' in *Let
the Whole Earth Hear His Voice*.

7. Clive Calver, *Sold Out* London, Marshall, Morgan & Scott 1980.

8. Clive Calver and Steve Chilcraft with Peter Meadows and
Simon Jenkins, *Dancing in the Dark?* Oxford, Lynx 1994.

9. John P. Baker, 'The Local Church in the Purpose of God' in ed. John P. Baker, *Christ's Living Body* London, Coverdale 1973.
10. A. W. Tozer, *Of God and Men* USA, Christian Publications.

Chapter 4   All One in Christ

1. Paul Knitter, *No Other Name?* Basingstoke, Marshalls 1991.
2. Harold A. Netland in ed. Robert E. Coleman, *Trinity World Forum* Spring 1993 (Deerfield, Ill., 1993).
3. Roy Clements in 'Can Tolerance Become the Enemy of Christian Freedom' Part II, *Cambridge Papers*, Vol. 1, no. 3 (Cambridge, 1992).
4. Eds. J. Hick and P. Knitters, *The Myth of Christian Uniqueness* London SCM 1987.
5. John Dewit, *Another Way of Looking* Swindon, Bible Society 1990.
6. Peter Cotterell in *London Bible College Review* London 1989.
7. Anglican Consultative Council, *Towards a Theology for Inter-Faith Dialogue* London, Church House Publishing 1984.
8. John Stott, *The Authentic Jesus* Basingstoke, Marshalls 1992.
9. Cormac Murphy-O'Connor (1984).
10. Michael Green *Evangelism in the Early Church* London, Hodder & Stoughton 1974.
11. Inter Faith Network, *Living With People of Different Faiths and Beliefs* London, 1993.
12. R. T. France and A. McGrath, *Evangelical Anglicans: their role and influence in the church today* London, SPCK 1993.

Chapter 5   Fracture points

1. *The Sword and the Trowel*, August 1887.
2. *The Sword and the Trowel*, October 1887.
3. Lewis Carroll, *Through the Looking Glass*.

Chapter 8   Together for Truth

1. Clive Calver, *Sold Out* London, Marshall Pickering 1981.
2. Gavin Reid, *To Reach a Nation* London, Hodder & Stoughton 1987.
3. Taken from, Clive Calver, Ian Coffey, Peter Meadows, *Who do Evangelicals think they are?* London, Evangelical Alliance 1993.
4. John Stott, *What is An Evangelical?* London, CPAS 1977.
5. John Wesley, *The Letters of John Wesley.*
6. David Bebbington, *Evangelicalism in Modern Britain: A History from the 1730s to 1980s* London, Unwin Hyman 1989.
7. Gavin Reid, p. 171.
8. Neil Summerton, 'Evangelicals approaching a new millennium' in *Aware* magazine, January 1992.
9. Quoted by David Holloway, 'What is an Anglican Evangelical' in ed. Melvin Tinker, *Restoring the Vision: Anglican Evangelicals Speak Out* Eastbourne, March 1990.
10. Richard Hutcheson Jr., *Mainline Churches and the Evangelicals: A Challenging Crisis?* Atlanta, John Knox Press 1981.
11. See further, Derek Tidball, *Who Are the Evangelicals?*
12. Alister McGrath, *Evangelicalism and the Future of Christianity* Downers Grove, Ill., IVP 1995.
13. Ian Coffey, 'Forward Together' in eds. Steve Brady, Clive Calver, Harold Rowdon, *For Such a Time as This* London, Scripture Union 1996.
14. Alan Gibson, 'The Role of Separation' in eds. Steve Brady, Clive Calver, Harold Rowdon.
15. Derek Tidball, p. 8.

Chapter 9   The Futures of Evangelicalism

1. J. R. Green *Short History of the English People* Harper 1899, pp. 736–7.